CliffsNotes

Lawrence and Lee's
Inherit the Wind

By Suzanne Pavlos

IN THIS BOOK

- ■ Learn about the Life and Background of the Playwrights
- ■ Preview an Introduction to the Play
- ■ Explore themes, literary devices, and character development in the Critical Commentaries
- ■ Examine an in-depth Character Analyses
- ■ Acquire an understanding of the play with the Critical Essays
- ■ Reinforce what you learn with CliffsNotes Review
- ■ Find additional information to further your study in CliffsNotes Resource Center and online at www.cliffsnotes.com

IDG
BOOKS
WORLDWIDE

IDG Books Worldwide, Inc.
An International Data Group Company
Foster City, CA • Chicago, IL • Indianapolis, IN • New York, NY

About the Author

Suzanne Pavlos taught high school for seven years and is a freelance writer and editor. She is currently working on her Master's degree in social work at the State University of New York at Albany.

Publisher's Acknowledgments

Editorial

Project Editor: Tracy Barr

Acquisitions Editor: Greg Tubach

Glossary Editors: The editors and staff of Webster's New World Dictionaries

Editorial Administrator: Michelle Hacker

Production

Indexer: York Production Services, Inc.

Proofreader: York Production Services, Inc.

IDG Books Indianapolis Production Department

CliffsNotes™ Lawrence and Lee's *Inherit the Wind*

Published by
IDG Books Worldwide, Inc.
An International Data Group Company
919 E. Hillsdale Blvd.
Suite 400
Foster City, CA 94404

www.idgbooks.com (IDG Books Worldwide Web site)

www.cliffsnotes.com (CliffsNotes Web site)

Library of Congress Catalog Card No.: xx-xxxxx

ISBN: 0-7645-8554-1

Printed in the United States of America

10 9 8 7 6 5 4 3 2 1

1O/QZ/QV/QQ/IN

Distributed in the United States by IDG Books Worldwide, Inc.

Library of Congress Cataloging-in-Publication Data

Pavlos, Suzanne.
  CliffsNotes, Inherit the wind / by Suzanne Pavlos.
    p. cm.
  Includes bibliographical references and index.
  ISBN 0-7645-8554-1 (alk. paper)
  1. Lawrence, Jerome, 1915-Inherit the wind--Examinations--Study guides. 2. Lee, Robert Edwin, 1918 ---Examinations--Study guides. 3. Evolution in literature. 4. Law in literature. I. Title.
PS3523.A934I636 2000
812'.54--dc21   00–035028
                                                        CIP

Distributed by CDG Books Canada Inc. for Canada; by Transworld Publishers Limited in the United Kingdom; by IDG Norge Books for Norway; by IDG Sweden Books for Sweden; by IDG Books Australia Publishing Corporation Pty. Ltd. for Australia and New Zealand; by TransQuest Publishers Pte Ltd. for Singapore, Malaysia, Thailand, Indonesia, and Hong Kong; by Gotop Information Inc. for Taiwan; by ICG Muse, Inc. for Japan; by Intersoft for South Africa; by Eyrolles for France; by International Thomson Publishing for Germany, Austria and Switzerland; by Distribuidora Cuspide for Argentina; by LR International for Brazil; by Galileo Libros for Chile; by Ediciones ZETA S.C.R. Ltda. for Peru; by WS Computer Publishing Corporation, Inc., for the Philippines; by Contemporanea de Ediciones for Venezuela; by Express Computer Distributors for the Caribbean and West Indies; by Micronesia Media Distributor, Inc. for Micronesia; by Chips Computadoras S.A. de C.V. for Mexico; by Editorial Norma de Panama S.A. for Panama; by American Bookshops for Finland.

For general information on IDG Books Worldwide's books in the U.S., please call our Consumer Customer Service department at **800-762-2974.** For reseller information, including discounts and premium sales, please call our Reseller Customer Service department at **800-434-3422.**

For information on where to purchase IDG Books Worldwide's books outside the U.S., please contact our International Sales department at **317-596-5530** or fax **317-572-4002.**

For consumer information on foreign language translations, please contact our Customer Service department at **1-800-434-3422,** fax 317-572-4002, or e-mail rights@idgbooks.com.

For information on licensing foreign or domestic rights, please phone **+1-650-653-7098.**

For sales inquiries and special prices for bulk quantities, please contact our Order Services department at **800-434-3422** or write to the address above.

For information on using IDG Books Worldwide's books in the classroom or for ordering examination copies, please contact our Educational Sales department at **800-434-2086** or fax **317-572-4005.**

For press review copies, author interviews, or other publicity information, please contact our Public Relations department at **650-653-7000** or fax **650-653-7500.**

For authorization to photocopy items for corporate, personal, or educational use, please contact Copyright Clearance Center, 222 Rosewood Drive, Danvers, MA 01923, or fax **978-750-4470.**

is a registered trademark under exclusive license to IDG Books Worldwide, Inc. from International Data Group, Inc.

Table of Contents

809
L

How to Use This Book

CliffsNotes *Inherit the Wind* supplements the original work, giving you background information about the playwrights, an introduction to the play, a graphical character map, critical commentaries, expanded glossaries, and a comprehensive index. CliffsNotes Review tests your comprehension of the original text and reinforces learning with questions and answers, practice projects, and more. For further information on Jerome Lawrence, Robert E. Lee, and *Inherit the Wind,* check out the CliffsNotes Resource Center.

CliffsNotes provides the following icons to highlight essential elements of particular interest:

Reveals the underlying themes in the work.

Helps you to more easily relate to or discover the depth of a character.

Uncovers elements such as setting, atmosphere, mystery, passion, violence, irony, symbolism, tragedy, foreshadowing, and satire.

Enables you to appreciate the nuances of words and phrases.

Don't Miss Our Web Site

Discover classic literature as well as modern-day treasures by visiting the CliffsNotes Web site at www.cliffsnotes.com. You can obtain a quick download of a CliffsNotes title, purchase a title in print form, browse our catalog, or view online samples.

You'll also find interactive tools that are fun and informative, links to interesting Web sites, tips, articles, and additional resources to help you, not only for literature, but for test prep, finance, careers, computers, and Internet, too. See you at www.cliffsnotes.com!

LIFE AND BACKGROUND OF THE PLAYWRIGHTS

Jerome Lawrence

Jerome Lawrence Schwartz was born on July 14, 1915 in Cleveland, Ohio, to Samuel Schwartz, a printer, and Sarah Rogen Schwartz, a poet. During his high school and college years, Lawrence was a prolific reader, reading every play—from Greek drama to current comedies—that he could find in the Cleveland and Ohio State University libraries. He also loved the theater. Because live theater was not commonplace throughout the United States during the 1930s, he hitchhiked to New York City to experience it.

Education

Lawrence received his Bachelor of Arts degree from Ohio State University in 1937. He worked for a short time as a reporter and telegraph operator for the *Wilmington News Journal* and as an editor for the *New Lexington Daily News*. His work as a newspaperman supplied him with a great deal of writing material that he made use of in later years. Also in 1937, Lawrence moved to California and began work as an editor for KMPC radio station in Beverly Hills. In 1939, he accepted a position as a writer for Columbia Broadcasting System (CBS) in Los Angeles and New York, and he attended the University of California, Los Angeles graduate school.

Career

Lawrence met Lee in New York City in 1942, and their partnership, which was to prove long-lasting and successful, was formed. Lawrence joined the United States Army in the early 1940s and was co-founder of the Armed Forces Radio Service. Although the majority of Lawrence's work over the next five decades was in collaboration with Lee, he continued to write plays and books on his own, using his given name Jerome L. Schwartz, Jerome Lawrence, and other pseudonyms. Lawrence independently wrote *Actor: The Life and Times of Paul Muni* (1974), which has been hailed one of the best theater biographies of the twentieth century. Today, Lawrence lives in Malibu, California, and spends his time writing and teaching aspiring playwrights.

Robert Lee

Robert Edwin Lee was born to Claire Melvin Lee, an engineer, and Elvira Taft Lee, a teacher, on October 15, 1918. He grew up in Elyria, Ohio. Lee married Janet Waldo, an actress, in 1948; together they had two children, Jonathan Barlow and Lucy Virginia. Lee died on July 8, 1994, in Los Angeles.

Education

Intent on becoming an astronomer, Lee attended Northwestern University in 1934 and then transferred to Ohio Wesleyan University, which (with Ohio State University) operated a giant telescope at Perkins Observatory. Interested in communications, Lee also immersed himself in broadcasting. He studied at Western Reserve University and Drake University in the late 1930s. Lee worked at the Perkins Observatory at Ohio Wesleyan while attending school there; then, while attending Western Reserve University, he worked for a radio station in Ohio.

Career

In the late 1930s, Lee moved to New York City to join an advertising firm. Lee met Lawrence in 1942 and, like Lawrence, spent time in the United States Army in the early 1940s. He was co-founder of the Armed Forces Radio Service. After being discharged from the Army, Lee continued his work with Lawrence. Although he wrote on his own, Lee's most well known work was written in collaboration with Lawrence.

Their Partnership and Work

Even though Lawrence and Lee had grown up only about thirty miles from each other, they did not meet until 1942 in New York City, where they formed a partnership to write and direct plays. Both men joined the army in 1942, temporarily suspending their professional collaboration. Their partnership resumed, however, after they returned home. Combining their talents, Lawrence and Lee wrote a myriad of plays and musicals, screenplays, radio plays, and scripts for radio and television programs, as well as stories and articles for various publications, biographies, and textbooks. Their partnership proved fulfilling, successful, and enduring and lasted until Lee's death in 1998.

In their work, Lawrence and Lee wanted to make people think about mankind and react to the world around them. They were relentless in their determination to fight limitations placed on the individual mind—limitations such as censorship, fear of what others would think, and bigotry.

Major Themes

Lawrence and Lee's passion for the freedom to think and the freedom to experience life is reflected in their work. Their protagonists, whether funny or serious, embody this philosophy. Drummond, in *Inherit the Wind,* shows audiences that differing perspectives must—and can—be valued with an open-mind. In *Auntie Mame,* Mame's curiosity enables her to live beyond the limitations that most women of that era faced. In *The Night Thoreau Spent in Jail,* Thoreau suffered the consequences for willfully violating what he considers to be unjust laws.

Literary Influences

Lawrence and Lee claim to have been influenced by playwrights such as Clifford Odets, Thornton Wilder, Lillian Hellman, Robert Sherwood, and others. Maxwell Anderson's work also had a significant impact on their work, particularly with *Inherit the Wind.* Anderson's play *Winterset* concerns the Sacco-Vanzetti trial in which two men are convicted of murder and sentenced to die, only to be found innocent after their executions. In *Winterset,* Anderson used dramatic license to add to the original case and to eliminate facts that he considered irrelevant to his play. He also made the conflict (social injustice) universal and timeless. Lawrence and Lee adapted this style when they wrote *Inherit the Wind.* Like Anderson, they used dramatic license to create a play based on a conflict that, at its heart, is both universal and timeless.

Honors and Awards

Together, Lawrence and Lee wrote an amazing amount of work. Many of their plays—*Inherit the Wind* (1955), *Auntie Mame* (1956) and *Mame* (1966) (the musical onstage version of *Auntie Mame*), *The*

Night Thoreau Spent in Jail (1970), and *First Monday in October,* (1975)—have been hailed as contemporary classics and been translated and performed in over thirty languages. Their work has received much critical acclaim and been honored with numerous awards, including the following:

- Two George Foster Peabody awards for distinguished achievement in broadcasting (1949 and 1952)

- The Donaldson Award for best new play (1955) for *Inherit the Wind*

- The *Variety* Critics Poll award, both in New York (1955) and London (1960), for *Inherit the Wind*

- The Lifetime Achievement Award from the American Theatre Association (1979)

- The Writers Guild of America Valentine Davies Award (1984) for contributions to the entertainment industry that have brought honor and dignity to all writers

In 1990, Lawrence and Lee were inducted into the Theater Hall of Fame and received membership in the College of Fellows of the American Theatre.

Other Contributions

In addition to their great plays, Lawrence and Lee made numerous other contributions to the theatre. They were co-founders of the Margo Jones Award and American Playwrights Theatre. Lawrence is a member of the Authors League of America and the Dramatists Guild, and Lee was a member of the Writers Executive Committee of the Academy of Motion Picture Arts & Sciences. Throughout the years, Lawrence and Lee shared a deep commitment to teaching, and taught and lectured extensively throughout the United States and abroad.

INTRODUCTION TO THE PLAY

Introduction

Lawrence and Lee wrote *Inherit the Wind* nearly thirty years after the Scopes Monkey trial. Although the basis of the play is the Scopes trial, the play itself is not a historical retelling of the events. Instead, the play is fiction. Each of the two main characters, Matthew Harrison Brady and Henry Drummond, represents one side of the central conflict: Brady represents the fundamentalist viewpoint, and Drummond is the advocate for science and freedom of thought. The courtroom battle that ensues between these famous attorneys is the focus of the play.

The Butler Act

After World War I, American society changed dramatically. The economy was thriving, the stock market was booming, and consumerism was at an all-time high. In addition, people migrated from rural to urban areas, leaving the conservative farmers with dwindling power. These changes fostered an atmosphere in which time-honored mores were questioned. Modernists—those who adapt their faith to contemporary trends in the sciences, philosophy, and history—embraced the changes taking place in America. Fundamentalists, on the other hand—those who believe in a literal interpretation of the Bible—clung to traditional beliefs.

Amidst the fast pace of the 1920s, people sought stability and fought to maintain a conservative lifestyle; as a result, the fundamentalist movement experienced a revival. Fundamentalists turned their attention to issues regarding the infallibility of the Bible in matters concerning science and history. Their focus became Darwin's theory of evolution, which espouses that species evolved over time through natural selection—a theory that is in direct opposition to the fundamentalist belief in the Biblical story of creation. Although teaching evolution in public schools was standard practice in the 1920s, fundamentalists initiated a movement to stop what they considered to be heretical teaching (that is, teaching that differed from their beliefs) and encouraged legislators to pass laws forbidding the teaching of evolution in public schools.

In 1921, John Washington Butler, a successful farmer in Tennessee, feared that the theory of evolution was influencing young people and crippling their religious beliefs. Firmly believing that the Bible was the foundation for American government and that anyone who disagreed was guilty of weakening the principles of the nation, Butler vowed to oppose the teaching of evolution in the public schools in Tennessee. He was elected to the Tennessee legislature in 1922 and was reelected in 1924. During his second term, he wrote his infamous anti-evolution act. The Butler Act, which sought to prohibit the teaching of evolutionary theory in all public schools in Tennessee, passed the Tennessee House of Representatives and the Tennessee Senate by solid majorities. On March 21, 1925, the governor of Tennessee, Austin Peay, signed the Butler Act into law.

The constitutionality of the Butler anti-evolution law was soon tested. John Scopes, a public school teacher, was arrested for teaching evolution. In Dayton, Tennessee, in July 1925, in the case *Tennessee v. John Thomas Scopes* (also known as "The Monkey Trial"), he was tried, convicted, and fined for violating the law.

The Scopes Trial

Upon hearing of the Butler Law, which prohibited the teaching of evolutionary theory in Tennessee's public schools, the American Civil Liberties Union (ACLU) in New York, a union that defends constitutional freedoms, sought to test the constitutionality of the law. It advertised in Tennessee newspapers for a teacher willing to challenge the law and offered to pay all trial expenses.

George Rappleyea, a Rhea County businessman and evolutionist, saw the ACLU's advertisement. He knew that such a test case would attract national attention, resulting in economic opportunities for the somewhat depressed Rhea County/Dayton area. Rappleyea spoke to other community leaders about the ACLU offer, and they agreed that a trial generating national attention would benefit the economy of Rhea County.

Rappleyea and the other town leaders summoned before them John Scopes, a 24 year-old science teacher and coach at the local high school who had substituted for the biology teacher during the last weeks of school. Scopes told the town leaders that, while substituting, he used a textbook entitled *A Civic Biology*, which contained evolutionary theory. The town leaders informed Scopes of the Butler Law and asked whether he would be willing to challenge the law. Scopes agreed, and within a short time, the town constable arrested him. Afterwards, Scopes, who was never jailed, returned to the tennis game from which he had been summoned.

Rappleyea sent a telegram to the ACLU informing them of Scopes' arrest; other town leaders notified Tennessee newspapers. Reporters arrived in Dayton from all over the United States and the world. The Baltimore *Sun* sent H.L. Mencken, a famous columnist known for his cynicism and wit, to cover the trial. The *Sun* also offered to pay Scopes' fine if he was found guilty.

Media focus on Scopes' arrest attracted the attention of William Jennings Bryan, a three-time presidential candidate, great orator, and fundamentalist who volunteered to prosecute the case. When Clarence Darrow, agnostic and famous criminal attorney, learned that Bryan was involved in Scopes case, he volunteered to defend Scopes. He realized that the case was no longer about Scopes' guilt or innocence; instead it was a battle between fundamentalism and freedom of thought. The trial began on July 10, 1925. The courtroom overflowed with spectators and reporters and radio microphones from WGN in Chicago. This event marked the first time a trial was covered by a radio broadcast.

Bryan and Darrow selected a jury that was composed of all white middle-aged men who were farmers, poorly educated, and church goers. After objections by Darrow to beginning each day's proceedings with a prayer, the prosecution began its case and quickly established that Scopes broke the law by teaching evolution in a public classroom. The defense had prepared its case around the testimony of expert witnesses on science and evolutionary theory. The judge, however, ruled the experts' testimony inadmissible. Most of the reporters, including H.L. Mencken, considered the trial to be over except for closing arguments, which would take place the following Monday. Assuming that the closing arguments would be uneventful, they left Dayton and missed the "battle of the century."

On Monday, when the trial resumed, Darrow switched his tactics. Instead of experts on evolutionary theory and science, he called an expert on the Bible to the stand—prosecuting attorney, William Jennings Bryan. Assuming that he would have an opportunity to cross-examine Darrow, Bryan cooperatively took the stand. In his questioning, Darrow sought to portray Bryan as an ignorant bigot and, in fact, got Bryan to admit that he did not interpret the Bible literally, a basic tenet of fundamentalism. At this admission, the spectators' support swayed to Darrow's side, and the judge halted the questioning.

The following day, the judge ordered that Bryan's testimony be stricken from the record as irrelevant to Scopes' guilt or innocence. To prevent Bryan from giving a closing speech, Darrow requested that the jury find Scopes guilty, which it did in fewer than ten minutes of deliberation. Bryan won the trial, but Darrow and Scopes won a moral victory. Five days after the conclusion of the trial, Bryan died in his sleep.

The judge fined Scopes $100; however, because the conviction was eventually overturned on a technicality, Scopes did not have to pay the fine. Despite the expectations of the combatants, the trial did not address the constitutionality of the Butler Act, which remained a state law in Tennessee until its repeal in 1967.

The Play and the Trial: How They Compare

Although Lawrence and Lee used the Scopes trial as the basis for their play, *Inherit the Wind* is a work of fiction. In their introduction, Lawrence and Lee make clear that the play is not history. "Some of the characters of the play are related to the colorful figures in the battle of giants; but they have life and language of their own—and, therefore, names of their own." The names Lawrence and Lee chose for their main characters are similar in sound and number of syllables to those who participated in the Scopes trial: William Jennings Bryan is now Matthew Harrison Brady. Clarence Darrow is Henry Drummond. John Scopes has become Bert Cates. And, H.L. Mencken of the Baltimore *Sun* is E.K. Hornbeck of the Baltimore *Herald*. The characterizations of all but one character, that of E.K. Hornbeck, however, bear no resemblance to the participants of the Scopes trial. The following illustrates other differences between the play and the trial.

The Scopes trial took place in Dayton, Tennessee, in July 1925 The play takes place in the "summer, in a small town (Hillsboro, Tennessee) not too long ago."

The Scopes trial originated when the American Civil Liberties Union (ACLU) in New York placed an advertisement in Tennessee newspapers offering to pay the expenses of a teacher willing to test the new anti-evolution law. The goal of the ACLU was to repeal the Butler Law. Dayton community leaders responded to the ACLU's announcement for economic reasons. They assumed the publicity of the trial would attract business and industry and would "put Dayton on the map." In the play, there are no ulterior reasons for the trial in Hillsboro. A man is simply arrested for breaking the law.

John T. Scopes, who was well-liked by Dayton community members, volunteered to be arrested for teaching evolution to test the constitutionality of the Butler Law, and he was never jailed. After his arrest, he was freed on $1,000 bond. His counterpart in the play, Bert Cates, is arrested for teaching evolution to his sophomore science class and is imprisoned throughout the duration of the trial. Furthermore, he is treated unkindly by the people of Hillsboro, as though he "has horns growing out of his head" and is "a pariah in the community."

Scopes did not request an attorney. When Darrow heard that Bryan would be assisting with the prosecution, he volunteered to serve as Scopes' attorney. In the play, Cates writes to a Baltimore newspaper to request an attorney, and the Baltimore *Herald* sends Drummond to Hillsboro to defend Cates.

The people of Dayton were portrayed as charming, friendly, polite, and open-minded, and the atmosphere throughout the trial is festive and circus-like. The citizens of Hillsboro, however, are portrayed as rude, narrow-minded religious fanatics. Although the atmosphere in Hillsboro is circus-like, it is sinister.

Bryan has been described as a great orator and politician, as well as a deeply religious man opposed to Darwin's theories, of which he was familiar. He was a charming, sincere, courteous man, despite his arrogance. Bryan handled himself well during the trial and was not out to persecute Scopes. In fact, Bryan offered to pay Scopes' fine if Scopes was found guilty. Bryan was also courteous and kind to witnesses. Brady, on the other hand, is a gifted orator and politician who enjoys hearing himself speak and thrives on being the center of attention. He is manipulative and condescending toward witnesses who don't believe as he does. As a fundamentalist and a self-proclaimed expert on the Bible, his mission is to defend the common man from "Evil-ution" and to make an example of Cates. He is also arrogantly foolish, pompous, and a glutton, and the great regard that the people of Hillsboro have for him identifies him as a man opposed to freedom of thought.

Clarence Darrow, a brilliant trial attorney who defended the underdog, had a hostile demeanor and was sarcastic and condescending. He volunteered to defend Scopes in order to expose the ignorance of fundamentalists. His counterpart in the play, Henry Drummond, is sophisticated, intelligent, idealistic, and charming.

When Darrow arrived in Dayton, a large, friendly crowd welcomed him. The welcome he received was similar to that which Bryan received. When Drummond arrives in Hillsboro, however, he does not receive a welcome. Instead, a young girl sees him and screams, "It's the Devil!"

Darrow objected to the Judge opening each session of the trial with a prayer and to a banner outside the courthouse that read, "Read Your Bible." He requested that the banner be taken down or another banner, one that read "Read Your Evolution," be erected. The judge had the banner removed. In the play, Drummond objects to the judge announcing a prayer meeting and to the banner outside the courthouse that says, "Read Your Bible." He, like Darrow, requests that the banner be taken down or that another banner—this one reading "Read Your Darwin"—be erected. Nothing is done about the banner.

In the Scopes trial, no women participated. In *Inherit the Wind,* Brady (the prosecutor) calls Rachel Brown to testify against Cates. (Note: John Scopes had no girlfriend. The playwrights included the character of Rachel to establish a romance motif.)

In the Scopes trial, Bryan agreed to take the witness stand because he thought he would have the opportunity to interrogate the defense afterward. In the play, Brady takes the witness stand to defend his fundamentalist position.

Darrow requested that Scopes be found guilty so that he could then appeal to a higher court to test the constitutionality of the Butler Law. By requesting the guilty verdict, he also avoided being cross-examined by Bryan and closing arguments. In the play, Drummond does not request a guilty verdict.

Bryan died in his sleep five days after the trial. Upon hearing of his death, Darrow commented that he "died of a busted belly." In *Inherit the Wind,* Brady collapses and dies as he tries to give his closing argument, and Darrow's famous words go to Hornbeck, who says that Brady "died of a busted belly."

The ACLU paid for all Scopes' expenses relating to the trial, and his teaching position was still open to him (he opted to attend graduate school instead, however). Cates, on the other hand, loses his job.

A Response to McCarthyism

Lawrence and Lee use *Inherit the Wind* as a metaphor for censorship or thought control; the play is their response to McCarthyism. Although the basis of the play is a historical event. the playwrights are not referring only to the Scopes trial (1925), the Butler Law, and the creationism-evolutionism conflict. They are also referring to the McCarthy era (the late 1940s and 1950s). *Inherit the Wind* was first published and produced in 1955, when blacklisting and, sometimes, imprisonment of Americans suspected of being members of the Communist party were at their height.

Wisconsin Senator Joseph R. McCarthy led an effort to identify Communists, who, he claimed, had infiltrated the federal government by the hundreds. During this period, the U.S. House of Representatives formed the Un-American Activities Committee (HUAC), in front of which American citizens were subpoenaed and forced to testify against or identify Communists. Because of their influence over American values, many people from the entertainment industry were called to testify, and several who were suspected of having connections to communism were blacklisted (denied employment because of their "unacceptable" opinions).

A Brief Synopsis

As *Inherit the Wind* opens, Bert Cates, having been arrested for teaching evolution to his sophomore science class, is in jail. Rachel Brown, his girlfriend and the daughter of Reverend Brown (the spiritual leader of Hillsboro) visits him. Rachel is confused and torn between the opposing beliefs held by Cates (academic freedom) and her father (fundamentalism) and her love for both of them. Desperately wanting to avoid the mounting controversy over his case, she pleads with Cates to admit he was wrong to teach evolution, and she is disappointed that Cates refuses.

Cates is nervous and frightened because he has learned that Matthew Harrison Brady, three-time presidential candidate, fundamentalist, and leader of the crusade against evolution, has volunteered to be the prosecuting attorney. He reveals to the bailiff, Mr. Meeker, that he has sent a letter to the Baltimore *Herald* asking for an attorney to defend him.

To celebrate Brady's arrival, the townspeople of Hillsboro carry posters, hang banners, provide a picnic lunch "fitt'n fer a king," and parade through the town singing "Gimme that old-time religion." Brady basks in the adoration of his followers and vows to defend the people of Hillsboro against "Evil-ution." E.K. Hornbeck, cynical columnist for the Baltimore *Herald*, also arrives in Hillsboro. He openly mocks Brady and is contemptuous of the bigotry and ignorance he observes in Hillsboro. He informs Brady's followers that Henry Drummond, an attorney famous for successfully defending underdogs, has been sent by the Baltimore *Herald* to defend Cates. Drummond arrives in Hillsboro later that evening. Upon his arrival, the only attention he receives is from Melinda, a young girl who screams that he's the devil.

When the trial begins, the courtroom is full. Both Brady and Drummond are self-assured: Brady, because he has the support of the spectators and is confident that his fundamentalist views are right and will, therefore, prevail; Drummond, because he seeks the truth.

After the first day in court, which involves selecting the jury, Reverend Brown holds a prayer meeting, at which he delivers a fire-and-brimstone sermon. Becoming overzealous, he prays that Cates be destroyed. When his daughter, Rachel, tries to stop him, he condemns her as well. Uncomfortable with the tenor of the prayer and afraid that Reverend Brown's actions may hinder the support the townspeople have in him, Brady steps forward and curtails Reverend Brown's sermon by reciting the wisdom of Solomon.

The following day, the trial proceeds and witnesses are called. Cates' students testify, and Rachel, whom Brady tricked into revealing confidential conversations she'd had with Cates, also testifies. The judge excludes Drummond's scientific witnesses claiming that evolution itself is not on trial. Determined to challenge the Butler Law, Drummond shrewdly switches his tactics and calls Brady to testify as an expert on the Bible. Brady arrogantly and ignorantly agrees to take the stand. Drummond's cross-examination of Brady, in which he exposes that Brady doesn't interpret the Bible literally and destroys Brady's credibility by questioning his status as a self-anointed prophet, changes the course of the trial.

The jury finds Cates guilty, and he is fined $100. Brady protests the minimal punishment. Although he won the case, his victory is a hollow one. The real triumph belongs to Drummond and Cates, who win a moral victory for freedom of thought.

Trying to stem the tide of attention and support that has rapidly drifted away from him, Brady insists on giving his closing speech, despite the fact that court had been adjourned and carnival atmosphere has intruded. Only a few of the faithful followers seem prepared to listen; the others who remain listen only grudgingly. Brady begins his speech, but he is unable to hold the crowd's attention. The final insult occurs when the radio announcer interrupts Brady to return the listeners to their regularly scheduled broadcast. Brady collapses, is removed from the courtroom, and soon after dies.

Rachel enters the courtroom, carrying a suitcase. She apologizes to Cates for her lack of understanding and to Drummond for possibly offending him. She reveals that she has read Darwin's *On Origin of Species,* and, although she doesn't like the premise of evolutionary theory, she now understands how important having the freedom to think is. She chooses to support Cates and leave her father.

Hornbeck continues to mock Brady after learning of his death, and Drummond defends Brady, angrily pointing out that "Brady had the same right as Cates: the right to be wrong!" Then Drummond leaves the courtroom with a Bible and a copy of Darwin's *On the Origin of Species.*

List of Characters

Matthew Harrison Brady The prosecuting attorney. He is a talented orator and an experienced politician. He is a defender of fundamentalism and a self-proclaimed expert on the Bible. He is pompous and self-righteous and is reduced to a tragic figure and ultimately dies after Drummond questions him on the witness stand.

Henry Drummond The defense attorney engaged by the Baltimore *Herald* for Cates. Drummond is sophisticated, charming, and idealistic. When he defends Cates, he is defending the freedom of thought and "the right to be wrong."

E.K. Hornbeck A newspaper columnist for the Baltimore *Herald* who is sent to Hillsboro to cover Cates' trial. Throughout the trial, he mocks Brady and his fundamentalist beliefs and the people of Hillsboro for their ignorant views about evolution.

Bertram Cates The defendant in the trial, a quiet, modest 24-year-old science teacher who has been arrested for teaching evolution to his sophomore science class.

Reverend Jeremiah Brown A fundamentalist preacher. As the spiritual leader of Hillsboro, he zealously believes in the literal interpretation of the Bible and is cruel and controlling.

Rachel Brown A 22-year-old second-grade schoolteacher who is the daughter of Reverend Jeremiah Brown and a close friend of Cates. Rachel experiences personal growth through the course of the play.

Judge The judge in Cates' trial. He tries to remain impartial in spite of his religious beliefs.

Mrs. Brady Brady's wife. She mothers her husband, watching over his health and diet.

Meeker The bailiff at the Hillsboro courthouse for many years. He is nonjudgmental and kind to Cates.

Melinda Loomis A 12-year -old girl. Upon seeing Drummond, she screams that he's the devil.

Howard Blair A student in Cates' science class. He testifies against Cates.

Mr. Goodfellow The owner of a general store near the courthouse. He is more interested in running his business than in the arrival of Brady or the upcoming trial.

Mrs. Krebs A member of the Hillsboro community. She plans a community picnic for the celebration of Brady's arrival and voices her opinions in the courtroom during the trial.

Corkin A local man who helps put up the banner that says, "Read Your Bible."

Bollinger, Cooper, Platt Local men who await Brady's train.

Mr. Bannister A local man who is selected to be a member of the jury.

Mrs. McClain A local woman who sells frond fans to people in the crowd awaiting the arrival of Brady's train.

Mrs. Loomis Melinda's mother.

Hawker A local man who sells hot dogs to the crowd awaiting Brady's arrival.

Mrs. Blair Howard's mother. She is a member of the Bible League and marches in the parade when Brady arrives.

Elijah A hermit. He sells Bibles and voices his religious beliefs to the crowd of people awaiting Brady's train. He tries to sell a Bible to Hornbeck.

Hurdy Gurdy Man An organ grinder, accompanied by his monkey, who waits with the crowd of people for Brady's arrival.

Timmy A young boy who excitedly announces to the crowd of people that Brady's train is coming.

Mayor The mayor of Hillsboro. He gives a speech welcoming Brady and bestows upon him the title of Honorary Colonel in the State Militia.

Photographer The photographer who takes pictures of Brady, the Mayor, and Reverend Brown during the welcoming ceremony.

Tom Davenport District Attorney who assists Brady during the trial.

Jesse H. Dunlap A farmer and cabinetmaker who is interviewed but rejected for jury duty.

George Sillers A man on the jury.

Reuter's Man A reporter from Reuters News Agency.

Harry Y. Esterbrook A radioman from WGN a radio station in Chicago.

Character Map

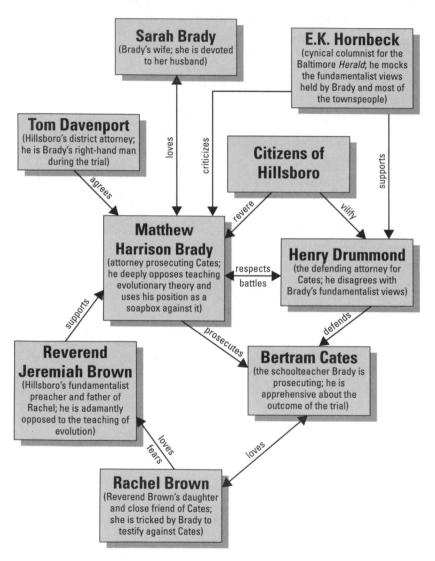

CRITICAL COMMENTARIES

Act I, Scene 1

Summary

The setting is Hillsboro, a small rural Tennessee town, during the summer of an unknown year. Bert Cates, a sophomore science teacher, has been arrested and jailed for violating the Butler Law, which prohibits the teaching of evolutionary theory in public schools. Rachel Brown, a fellow teacher and his girlfriend, pleads with him to apologize and admit that he was wrong. Cates, however, refuses to give up.

The townspeople are excited because Matthew Harrison Brady, three-time presidential candidate, famous orator, and fundamentalist leader, is arriving in Hillsboro to join the district attorney, Tom Davenport, in prosecuting Cates. The atmosphere of the town is similar to that of a country fair. Banners are flying and people are selling lemonade, hot dogs, and Bibles. The Ladies' Aid has prepared a picnic for Brady and his wife, Sarah, and everyone is in a festive mood. During the celebration, Brady discovers that Rachel Brown, the daughter of the spiritual leader of Hillsboro, Reverend Jeremiah Brown, is a friend of Cates. He tricks her into revealing confidential, incriminating conversations she and Cates have had.

At the picnic, E.K. Hornbeck, a cynical columnist from the Baltimore *Herald*, reveals to Brady and the townspeople that famous defense attorney Henry Drummond will be Cates' attorney. This news shocks everyone, and Reverend Brown compares Drummond to the devil. Later that evening, Drummond arrives in Hillsboro alone.

Commentary

Theme

In this scene, Lawrence and Lee supply the facts needed to understand the play. They use Hillsboro, a town that is " . . . about to be vigorously awakened," as a symbolic representation of people getting along in life without getting involved. Laws that encourage censorship are passed (specifically the Butler Law), and freedoms slip away. The people of Hillsboro live their lives in a vacuum, not thinking about the consequences of such a law until Cates' arrest. Cates' trial awakens the people of Hillsboro to the notion that there is no right or wrong way to think, that the important thing is having the freedom to think and being able to exercise that freedom.

In the first scene, Lawrence and Lee establish the central conflict of the play—the controversy between evolutionism and creationism—and introduce the characters involved in the conflict. Thus, the play begins with the interaction between Howard and Melinda, young people who live in Hillsboro. Melinda tells Howard he talks "sinful," and Howard calls Melinda's father a monkey. Their interaction foreshadows disharmony among community members regarding, specifically, the issues of evolutionism and creationism, but more globally, the issues of freedom of thought and censorship.

The stage directions emphasize the importance of the crowd as "active spectators." The crowd, made up of townspeople, provides dramatic tension throughout the play. In this scene, the townspeople are in high spirits because Matthew Harrison Brady is coming to Hillsboro to prosecute Cates, a minor character in the play who represents John Scopes. The townspeople have created a circus-like atmosphere. The town is decorated, food and other items are being sold, people sing and carry anti-evolution banners, and a band is ready to play.

The southern dialect spoken by the townspeople is realistic. They anticipate that, when Brady arrives, the "town's gonna fill up like a rain barrel in a flood," and they wonder, "where we gonna sleep all them people?" The Ladies Aid has even prepared a picnic that's, "Fitt'n fer a king." Clearly showing their support for Brady and his position against evolution, the townspeople sing, "Gimme that old-time religion," as Brady steps off the train. Lawrence and Lee's use of dialect and their portrayal of most of the citizens of Hillsboro reveal the townspeople as ignorant and unsophisticated—a typical stereotype of the rural South.

When Brady arrives in Hillsboro with his doting wife, Sarah, he assumes the role of leader of the common people. He is opposed to evolution and, during his arrival speech and later at the picnic, assures the townspeople that he is in Hillsboro to "defend . . . the Living Truth of the Scriptures," and "to test the steel of (his) Truth against the blasphemies of Science." According to Hornbeck, Brady is actually in Hillsboro "to find himself a stump to shout from. That's all." Brady's ambition is to boost his popularity in the eyes of his followers, and he is on a crusade against evolution, similar to McCarthy's crusade against Communism in the 1950s.

To emphasize Brady's determination, Lawrence and Lee use allusions (references to historical or famous people, objects, or events) to suggest more than what he is saying. Brady, for example, compares his battle to the battles of Goliath and St. George, which represent the defeat of an imposing, and presumably unconquerable, monster by an average man.

In their characterizations of Brady and Reverend Brown, Lawrence and Lee reveal their thoughts about people who promote censorship. Brady is a narrow-minded bigot who is opposed to evolutionary theory but knows nothing about it. Reverend Jeremiah Brown, the spiritual leader of Hillsboro and, like Brady, a strict fundamentalist, uses his position as a town leader to subjugate, or rule, the townspeople.

Lawrence and Lee portray Brown as a stereotypical fire-and-brimstone preacher. He is cruel and controlling. At the welcome picnic, Brown is adamant that his daughter, Rachel, speak to Brady about Cates, and after she does, he tells Brady that, "Rachel has always been taught to do the righteous thing." When Brown hears that Drummond is going to be Cates' defense attorney, he comments that Cates is "a vicious Godless man" who could be the " . . . Devil himself." His immediate reaction is to keep Drummond out of Hillsboro. In this dialogue, Lawrence and Lee hint at the fear that exists when people are not willing to acknowledge different beliefs.

E. K. Hornbeck, a cynical newspaper columnist for the Baltimore *Herald* who was sent to Hillsboro to cover Cates' trial, is also a character who has trouble accepting differing beliefs. Hornbeck, however, is not fundamentalist; he is pro-evolution and a champion of Cates.

Lawrence and Lee have written Hornbeck's dialogue in the form of poetry, making use of figurative language, such as metaphors, to draw comparisons and allusions. As such, Hornbeck functions as a *chorus character,* enabling Lawrence and Lee to moralize and relay social commentary to the audience. Hornbeck's cynical comments also provide comic relief throughout the play, thereby relieving tension. He tells a community member that he'd rather die than use a complimentary fan from a funeral home, and he welcomes a monkey to Hillsboro by exclaiming, "Grandpa!"

Mocking Brady, Hornbeck refers to him as a monkey's competition and alludes sarcastically to "the legions of the Lion-Hearted," referring to Brady's huge following. After announcing to the picnickers that Drummond will be defending Cates, Hornbeck, happy with the stir he creates, bids the townspeople, "A Merry Christmas and a Jolly Fourth of July!" His flippant comment—holidays celebrating the birth of Jesus Christ and the independence of the United States from Great Britain—foreshadows the enlightenment that the fundamentalists will experience.

Hornbeck goes to the courtroom to " . . . inspect the battlefield" and meets Rachel, who is quite distraught. Using allusions, he sarcastically refers to Baltimore as a "wicked Sodom and Gomorrah." He compares Cates to the "boy-Socrates, latter-day Dreyfus, Romeo with a biology book"—allusions that liken Cates to an enlightened mind that is unjustly persecuted. When he says to Rachel, "Wake up, Sleeping Beauty," he identifies her as someone who lives in a dream world and foreshadows her growth through the play.

Lawrence and Lee also use Hornbeck to emphasize the differences between the North and South. A sophisticated city-dweller from the North, Hornbeck is haughty and contemptuous of the ignorance and bigotry he observes in the South. Providing commentary to the audience at every opportunity, he mocks Hillsboro by calling the town "Heavenly Hillsboro" and claims that it is "the buckle on the Bible Belt," a town where "ignorance bushes" grow, but no "Tree of Knowledge."

Henry Drummond, Cates' defense attorney is also from the North. When he arrives in Hillsboro at the conclusion of Scene 1, he is alone and shunned by the townspeople. In fact, when Melinda, the little girl, sees him, she calls him a devil and runs from him. The only information that Lawrence and Lee reveal about Drummond up to this point is that he is an agnostic—that is, he doesn't believe that knowing whether God exists is possible—and he is a famous and skilled defense attorney. Lawrence and Lee also use Drummond as a mouthpiece to voice their views and concerns about limitations placed on an individual's right to think.

Drummond is a foil for Brady. The features of both Brady and Drummond are intensified by the presence of the other. For example, Brady's pompousness becomes magnified when juxtaposed with Drummond's low-key style. As Brady remarks, Drummond "magnifies our cause." The playwrights also use a romance motif, a conventional sub-plot, to relate and intensify Rachel Brown's internal conflict. Rachel, who loves Cates and whose father is Reverend Brown, struggles because she has been taught to believe that fundamentalism is the right and only belief to have. She pleas with Cates to "be on the right side of things" and then later defends him, telling Brady that he really is "good." Lawrence and Lee use Rachel's internal conflict to create suspense and to represent the opening of closed minds.

Glossary

(Here and in the following glossary sections, difficult words and phrases, as well as allusions and historical references, are explained.)

scorcher [Colloquial] a very hot day.

composition-paper suitcase a cheap cardboard suitcase.

vagrant a person who wanders from place to place without a regular job, supporting himself by begging, etc.

extradite to turn over (a person accused or convicted of a crime) to the jurisdiction of another country, state, etc. where the crime was allegedly committed.

Chautauqua meeting one of various late 19th and early 20th century meetings that were often held outdoors in tents and featured lectures, concerts, and plays, in addition to popular education.

rig to put together, prepare for use, or arrange, esp. in a makeshift or hurried fashion.

halyards a rope or tackle for raising or lowering a flag, sail, etc.

caricatured rubes unsophisticated people whose characteristics have been exaggerated.

Coxey's Army In 1894, Jacob Sechler Coxey (1854-1951), an entrepreneur, joined with Carl Browne, a revivalist, to lead a group of 500 unemployed people, a "living petition," from Massillon, Ohio, to Washington, D.C., in support of his plan for national reconstruction. The marchers became known as "Coxey's Army," and the demonstration when Coxey was arrested for demonstrating on the Capitol lawn.

hawker one who advertises or peddles (goods) in the streets by shouting.

hoist to raise aloft; lift or pull up, esp. by means of a cable, pulley, crane, etc.

toots a ragged fanfare plays a song on a trumpet or horn.

frond the leaf of a palm or fern.

privy a toilet; esp. an outhouse.

Bible Belt [coined (c.1925) by Henry Louis Mencken] those regions of the U.S., particularly areas in the South, where fundamentalist beliefs prevail and Christian clergy are especially influential.

Elijah a Hebrew prophet mentioned in the Old and New Testaments of the Bible.

monkeyshines [Colloquial] a mischievous or playful trick, joke, or prank.

Lion-Hearted Richard I (1157-1199), King of England. His courage in battle earned him the title of *Coeur de Lion* (Lion-Hearted).

county cooler a county jail.

pith helmet a light-weight hat made from the soft, spongy, tissue that is often worn in hot, humid climates.

suffrage the right to vote, esp. in political elections.

President Wilson (1856-1924), 28th president of the United States (1913-1921).

agape with the mouth wide open, in surprise, wonder, etc., gaping.

repast food and drink for a meal.

fit on the old armor prepare for battle.

heathen dogma a doctrine, tenet, or belief that does not relate to God or the Bible.

agnostic a person who believes that the human mind cannot know whether there is a God or an ultimate cause, or anything beyond material phenomena.

Goliath a gigantic Philistine warrior who taunted Israelis forces. Because of his large size, people were frightened of him. Finally, David fought Goliath with his sling and five smooth stones. He hit Goliath in the head causing him to fall and then took Goliath's sword and killed him.

St. George a figure in a legend similar to that of David and Goliath. In this legend, the only source of water for a great city was an oasis that was guarded by a dragon that would kill the youths who tried to get water. Finally, the king's daughter, the only youth left to try to get water, went to the oasis. St. George rode up on a white horse and killed the dragon with a lance. The king gave St. George half of his kingdom and his daughter's hand in marriage.

fray a noisy quarrel or fight; brawl.

Sodom and Gomorrah two cities mentioned in the Bible, well known for their wicked and inhospitable ways, that were destroyed by God. The cities are symbols of human sinfulness and God's punishment for such.

tear sheet a sheet torn, or taken in unbound form, from a publication for special distribution.

Happy Hooligan, Barney Google, and Abe Kabibble famous newspaper comic strips.

Socrates (469-399 B.C.) Greek philosopher and mentor of Plato. He developed the Socratic method of inquiry, based on reason and self-knowledge. He believed in doing what one thought was right, even if it meant facing the opposition of all others. Socrates was charged with impiety and corruption of youth and sentenced to death.

Dreyfus a scapegoat or one who is wrongly accused. Captain Alfred Dreyfus (1859-1935), a Jewish officer in the French Army, was accused of sending secret military documents to the German military. He was convicted of treason, court-martialed, and exiled. Later, it was discovered that Major Ferdinand Walsin Esterhazy, a Hungarian with German connections, was the guilty party. Dreyfus had been a convenient scapegoat. In 1906, he was proclaimed innocent.

Romeo a character from Shakespeare's *Romeo and Juliet*. A Montague, he was in love with the daughter of a Capulet, Juliet, enemy of his family.

Little Eva an angelic child in the novel *Uncle Tom's Cabin* (1851-1852) by Harriet Beecher Stowe. Of frail health, she dies. Also a possible reference to Eve, Adam's wife, in the Book of Genesis of the Bible.

Tree of Knowledge the tree in the Garden of Eden from which Adam and Eve ate.

hinterland an area far from big cities and towns; back country.

plumbing in their heads brains.

Henry's Lizzie Henry Ford's first automobile model, the Model T, also known as the "Tin Lizzie."

flivver a small, cheap automobile, esp. an old one.

Marconi Guglielmo Marconi (1874-1937), an Italian electrical engineer who invented the first radio-signaling system.

Montgomery Ward the oldest mail-order business in the United States, launched by Aaron Montgomery Ward in 1872.

Act I, Scene 2

Summary

Spectators crowd the hot courtroom several days later as Brady and Drummond choose the last two jurors for Cates' trial. Throughout the questioning, friction between Brady and Drummond becomes apparent as they haggle about every issue. Their bickering makes clear that this trial is *not* just about Cates' guilt or innocence but about censorship versus freedom of thought.

After the judge adjourns the trial for the day, Rachel Brown goes to Drummond and insists that he call off the trial. Cates reveals that he is scared but determined to stand his ground. Drummond admits that he cares about what Cates' thinks and is empathetic. Rachel feels confused, guilty, and upset. She tells Drummond and Cates that she talked to Brady about conversations she had had with Cates and will have to testify against him.

Commentary

Lawrence and Lee's purpose for this scene is to delineate each side of the conflict. With stage directions that state the situation is "as if Hillsboro itself is on trial," the playwrights suggest that the narrow-minded thinking that promotes censorship—thinking that is prevalent in Hillsboro—is on trial.

Literary Device

The prospective jurors that Drummond and Brady question are males who are not particularly well educated. Through the jury-selection process, the two attorneys challenge each other, revealing one another's strengths and weaknesses. Because Drummond is a foil for Brady, the men's differences are magnified whenever they are in each other's presence. Brady is self-assured and smug because he has the spectators on his side. Drummond, although alone in his fight to defend Cates, never wavers from his mission to defend academic freedom.

Lawrence and Lee portray Drummond as a sophisticated city dweller from the North, a sharp contrast to Brady and the simple townspeople living in the rural South. For example, Drummond exhibits a sense of humor about his purple suspenders, which incurs Brady's sarcasm about Drummond wearing the "latest fashion." Brady's self-importance is evident when the issue of his title as Honorary Colonel in the State Militia arises, and the audience sees that Brady is impressed with the title. Drummond, on the other hand, thinks the title is ridiculous and is mildly entertained when the mayor of Hillsboro gives him a *temporary* title of Honorary Colonel in the State Militia.

Character Insight

Drummond's character is revealed, as well as Lawrence and Lee's viewpoint, when he angrily responds to Brady's comment about wanting, " . . . the state of mind of the members of the jury [to] conform[s] to the laws and patterns of society." Drummond is passionate about " . . . prevent[ing] the clock-stoppers from dumping a load of medieval nonsense into the United States Constitution." The tension mounts as Drummond slaps his hand on the table vowing to, " . . . stop 'em somewhere."

Theme

Drummond believes that censorship halts progress and that a society in which limitations are placed on an individual's right to think is dangerous. In this passage, Drummond is voicing Lawrence and Lee's concern about censorship. Here, the playwrights are not commenting only on the Butler Law, but also on the censorship that occurred during the McCarthy era. McCarthyism forced people to conform to the "acceptable" ideology of capitalism and to abandon any connections to Communism or risk losing their jobs and possibly facing trial and imprisonment.

By defending Cates and freedom of thought, Drummond is shaking Hillsboro's very foundation. In response, the town attempts to hold on to its traditional fundamentalist beliefs. They erect a banner over the courtroom door that proclaims, "Read Your Bible," and, as court is adjourned for the day, the judge announces a prayer meeting to be held on the courthouse lawn. Drummond objects to the banner, as well as the "commercial announcement" of the prayer meeting, but the judge rules that he is out of order.

At the end of the day, Brady leaves the courtroom like "a shepherd leading his flock." Because his self-worth is based on the attention he receives from his followers, he thrives on being popular. In contrast, Drummond quietly packs his briefcase with Cates still at his side. When Rachel begs Drummond to call off the trial, he explains that challenging "an old wives' tale," a traditional belief, is a bigger crime than a murder because it shakes people up and causes them to think and make changes. Here, the playwrights emphasize the theme of the play—the right of every individual to think freely and to explore what is unknown and unfamiliar. Drummond's character is revealed in a monologue as he empathizes with Cates' alienation and loneliness. Drummond speaks as though he had a similar experience. In fact, Lawrence and Lee wrote a prequel to *Inherit the Wind* entitled *The Angels Weep,* in which Drummond is in a courtroom facing a judge as a *defendant* because of an unjust accusation.

In this scene, Lawrence and Lee use allusions to emphasize the character's dilemmas and the atmosphere of the town. When Cates says he never thought the trial would be "like Barnum and Bailey coming to town," he is alluding to the Barnum and Bailey Circus—The Greatest Show on Earth. The purpose of the allusion is to describe the circus-like atmosphere the townspeople have created. Yet, even though the atmosphere of Hillsboro appears to be festive, the underlying mood is sinister because the townspeople are defending their long-held fundamentalist beliefs against evolutionary theory. Another allusion occurs when Rachel reveals that she will be asked to testify against Cates. Reacting in disbelief and fear, he exclaims, " . . . they'll crucify me!"—words immediately conjuring up the image of the crucifixion of Jesus, a man who was betrayed by one of his disciples.

At the end of Scene 2, when Drummond reassures Rachel that Cates is not wicked and shows that he clearly supports Cates and respects his willingness to stand up for academic freedom, Lawrence and Lee illustrate that Drummond is not a devil, but a kind, compassionate, and caring person.

Glossary

venireman a member of a group of people from among whom a jury or juries will be selected.

clock-stoppers narrow-minded thinkers.

cold feet fright.

pariah any person despised or rejected by others; an outcast.

grip a small bag or satchel for holding clothes, etc. in traveling.

Act II, Scene 1

Summary

The same evening, the townspeople congregate on the courthouse lawn for Reverend Brown's prayer meeting. All the major characters are present, except for Cates. Brady sits on the wooden platform. Drummond and Hornbeck are at the edge of the crowd.

When Brown becomes overzealous as he prays and asks that Cates, as well as anyone who supports him (including his daughter, Rachel), be destroyed and damned, Brady interrupts him and ends the payer meeting. Left standing alone with Drummond, Brady questions him about their relationship, once cordial, and wonders why Drummond has "... moved so far away from me." Drummond tells Brady that perhaps he, Brady, is the one who has moved away " ... by standing still."

Commentary

Whereas at the end Act I Lawrence and Lee depict the evolutionists (primarily Drummond), in this first scene of Act II, they depict the people on the opposing side of the conflict—the fundamentalists. As the scene opens, Drummond, who in the last scene is shown to be caring and compassionate, is once again referred to as "the Devil" by workmen who decide to leave up the "Read your Bible" banner. The fundamentalist Brady casts Drummond as the enemy of the faithful when he concludes a press conference with reporters and proclaims that he is "fighting the fight of the Faithful throughout the world," while Drummond is "challenging the faith of millions."

Literary Device

As the townspeople congregate for the prayer meeting, the stage directions point out that "the prayer meeting is motion picture, radio, and tent-show to these people," and Reverend Brown is their movie star. Because the prayer meetings are obviously the only form of entertainment for the townspeople, attendance is high. Lawrence and Lee hint at the possibility that some of the townspeople may not truly be fundamentalists, foreshadowing a lack of support and ultimate devastation for Brady.

Brown bases his sermon on the creation story in the Bible. Lawrence and Lee use the creation story and Brown's sermon to both remind the audience of the creation story as it is told in the Bible and to illustrate how narrow-minded these anti-evolutionists are. In this scene, the playwrights mock not only the fundamentalists but also the people who participated in McCarthyism and anyone who favors censorship.

Character Insight

Lawrence and Lee portray Brown as an uncaring person who shows no compassion for another human being (Cates) or his own child (Rachel). When Brown prays fervently for Cates' destruction and Rachel cries out to stop him only to be condemned by him, too, Brady who is, above almost everything else, ambitious, becomes nervous. The people in the congregation are his supporters. Uncomfortable with the direction the sermon has taken and afraid that he will lose the people's support, Brady steps up to Brown and puts a halt to the prayer meeting. In so doing, he quotes from the Book of Proverbs, "he that troubleth his own house . . . shall inherit the wind," implying that those who cause problems get nothing in return. The prayer meeting comes to an end as Brady talks about forgiveness. Rachel leaves the prayer meeting in disbelief. Her internal struggle represents the struggle faced by anyone who becomes enlightened and is awakened to new knowledge. Rachel's love for Cates and her father's condemnation of her make her question what she has long believed to be true.

The playwrights also use this scene to clarify the relationship between Brady and Drummond. At one time, the two men were "on the same side of the fence"; they shared " . . . a mutuality of understanding and admiration." At the conclusion of Brown's prayer meeting, Brady questions Drummond about the distance that has come between them, and Drummond responds that "Perhaps it is *you* [Brady] who have moved away—by standing still."

Glossary

same side of the fence having the same beliefs.

dispatches news stories sent to a newspaper or broadcaster, as by a correspondent.

fervent having or showing great warmth of feeling; intensely devoted or earnest; ardent.

Milton Sills (1882-1930), a handsome silent film star well known for his leading roles in *The Spoilers, The Sea Hawk,* and *Burning Daylight.*

Douglas Fairbanks (1883-1939), a handsome silent film star, famous for his roles in *The Mark of Zorro, The Three Musketeers,* and *Robin Hood.*

milking the expectant pause taking advantage of a pause to prolong anticipation.

whipping'em up getting the crowd excited.

whip-crack quickly; forcefully; loud.

zeal intense enthusiasm, as in working for a cause; ardent endeavor or devotion; ardor; fervor.

Act II, Scene 2

Summary

Two days later, the trial is well underway. Howard, one of Cates' former students, takes the witness stand, followed by Rachel Brown. Because Rachel is obviously upset, Cates tells Drummond not to cross-examine her. When Drummond calls his scientific witnesses to the stand, Brady objects, and the judge determines the testimony of the scientific witnesses irrelevant and excludes them on the grounds that evolution itself is not on trial. Drummond then suggests putting Brady on the witness stand as an expert on the Bible. Brady gladly agrees. In his questioning of Brady, Drummond exposes that Brady, a strict fundamentalist, does not interpret the Bible literally and that he considers himself to be a prophet. The spectators laugh at Brady and leave the courtroom. Brady turns to his wife for comfort and support.

Commentary

This scene is the climactic scene in the play. While questioning Howard, a student in Cates' class, Brady seizes the opportunity to give a speech defending the Butler Law and the common people against "Evil-utionists," "Bible-haters," and "the teachings of Godless Science." He is confident as the spectators applaud, showing their support.

Character Insight

As Brady's foil, Drummond stands alone. The stage directions state that, " . . . the courtroom seems to resent . . ." his boldness and relaxed demeanor. Drummond is not in awe of Brady and does not hesitate to point out his flaws. Still, his intent is not to destroy Brady but to crush the narrow-minded thinking that Brady represents and promotes. The theme of the play, as well as Lawrence and Lee's viewpoint, is evident as Drummond cross-examines Howard, establishing that everyone "has the right to think."

When the judge says that " . . . the right to think is not on trial . . .," he is reminding Drummond—and the audience—that Hillsboro is a southern fundamentalist town. When Drummond asks Howard whether, simply because they are not mentioned in the Bible, modern conveniences are "sinful" or "instruments of the Devil," he is establishing that the Bible does not have all the answers. At this point, Brady accuses Drummond of confusing material things with "spiritual realities" and, consequently, confusing Howard. Brady makes clear that he is concerned with what is *right*. Drummond is explicit when he responds that *truth* is his main concern. Here, Lawrence and Lee foreshadow the future as Howard "stares at his newfound idol," Drummond.

Literary Device

As Rachel takes the witness stand, the stage directions comment that "Cates watches her with a hopeless expression: *Et tu, Brute.*" Lawrence and Lee allude to the line from Shakespeare's play *Julius Caesar,* in which Brutus betrays his close friend, Caesar. (When Brutus stabs Caesar, Caesar says, "*Et tu, Brute?*"—meaning, "and you too, Brutus?") When, during questioning, Rachel becomes so distraught that the power to speak eludes her, Cates asks Drummond not to question her, showing compassion, even though she has betrayed him. In contrast, Rachel's father "unsympathetically" walks her off the witness stand. Lawrence and Lee once again portray the fundamentalists as uncaring and cold people and the evolutionists as people who are concerned about the welfare of others.

Literary Device

The classical theme of *hubris* (excessive pride or self-confidence, which is essential to Greek tragedy) is evident in Brady's character at this point, showing him to be a tragic figure. His arrogance and pride cause him to ignore Davenport's objections to Drummond's unorthodox request and to foolishly take the witness stand in order to " . . . speak out . . . on behalf of the Living Truth of the Holy Scriptures." This act of hubris causes Brady to lose those things he holds most dear.

Theme

Drummond uses Brady's testimony to show that God intended man to think. When he is accused of being contemptuous of all that is holy, Drummond angrily responds that he believes that the "individual human mind" is holy and that "an idea is a greater monument than a cathedral." Drummond's monologue reveals his (as well as Lawrence and Lee's) passion about the value of the human mind and the importance of having the freedom to think.

The climax of the play occurs when Brady finally admits that he does not interpret the Bible literally and that he thinks of himself as a prophet. At this point, the spectators' support begins to shift from Brady to Drummond. By the time Brady admits that God talks to him, the spectators are laughing at his responses to Drummond's questions. This laughter is painful to Brady because he realizes that his followers are slipping away.

Desperate, Brady accuses Drummond of trying to "destroy everyone's belief in God." Drummond angrily replies that he is " . . . trying to stop you bigots and ignoramuses from controlling the education of the United States!" Drummond's reply is an expression of Lawrence and Lee's passion against censorship, not only in relationship to the Butler Law but to McCarthyism as well.

His credibility destroyed, Brady falls apart on the witness stand and, after Drummond excuses him, says to the crowd, "All of you know what I stand for! What I believe! I believe, I believe in the truth of the Book of Genesis!" and then, almost unthinkingly, begins to recite the names of the other Books of the Bible. Brady's former flock crowds around Drummond as he leaves the courtroom; Brady is left on the witness stand with his wife, who comforts him. The tone at the conclusion of this scene is somber.

Glossary

Revealed Word God's word.

fuss and feathers confusion.

southpaw [Slang] a person who is left-handed; esp., a left-handed baseball pitcher.

goop-eyed in awe.

fatuity stupidity, esp. complacent stupidity; smug foolishness.

hushed babble quiet confused, incoherent talk or vocal sounds.

relish anything that gives pleasure, zest, or enjoyment; attractive quality.

bully for you good for you.

precepts a commandment or direction meant as a rule of action or conduct.

pagan a person who is not a Christian, Muslim, or Jew; heathen; sometimes applied specifically to non-Christians by Christians.

perdition the loss of the soul; damnation; hell.

gall [Colloquial] rude boldness; impudence; audacity.

whoop up excite.

cocksure sure or self-confident in a stubborn or overbearing way.

cocks an eye looks.

scent in the wind understand what is going on that is not verbalized.

play in your ball park do as you want.

Jonah a minor prophet in the Book of Jonah in the Old Testament of the Bible.

Joshua Moses' successor. Joshua leads the Israelites across the River Jordan and engages in a series of battles to take Palestine. His story is told in the Book of Joshua found in the Old Testament of the Bible.

Houdini Harry Houdini (1874-1926) world famous magician.

Copernicus (1473-1543), a Polish astronomer known for his theory that the earth spins on its axis once daily and revolves around the sun (which is at rest near the center of the universe) annually.

Original Sin In the Old Testament of the Bible, Adam sinned by eating from the Tree of Knowledge. Because of Adam's fall, original sin is the state of sin that, according to Christian theology, characterizes all human beings.

sticks turned to snakes Biblical reference. Several times in the Bible, sticks or staffs are turned into snakes.

parting of waters reference to Moses' parting the Red Sea (Exodus 14:15). When Moses brought the Israelites out of Egypt, God told him to raise his staff and stretch his hand over the sea to divide the water.

Rock of Ages Israelite faith considered God, figuratively, to be a rock, symbolizing the permanence and stability of divine protection. The *Rock of Ages* (1774) is a hymn written by a Calvinist Anglican minister Augustus M. Toplady.

die-hard stubborn or resistant person, esp. an extreme conservative.

glib gag a practical joke or hoax spoken in a smooth, fluent, easy manner, often in a way that is too smooth and easy to be convincing.

trap is about to be sprung someone is about to be caught in someone else's scheme.

Act III

Summary

The next day, everyone returns to the courtroom to hear the verdict, which is to be broadcast on WGN radio station. Cates is found guilty and is fined $100. In his statement to the court, he vows to continue to oppose the Butler Law. Brady has won the case but does not feel victorious. The spectators no longer view him as their illustrious leader; they have turned their backs on him. Drummond is triumphant in his fight for freedom of thought. Brady attempts to make his closing speech after the judge has adjourned the court, but the spectators leave, ignoring Brady's efforts to hold their attention. He collapses and dies soon after. Rachel and Cates leave Hillsboro together.

Commentary

This act comprises the falling action and the catastrophe of the play. The tone is grim, and the anticipation mounts as everyone awaits the verdict of the trial. Hornbeck provides comic relief as he gives a commentary on his interpretation of the action. He asks if the jury is out "swatting flies and wrestling with justice—in that order." And then he sarcastically remarks that he will "hate to see the jury filing in" because he will "miss Hillsboro."

Literary Device

Using a metaphor, Lawrence and Lee speak through Drummond to describe the necessity of seeking truth. Drummond comments that when the people of Tennessee "started this fire" (passed the Butler Law), they never thought it would "light up the whole sky" (create national attention). "People's shoes are getting hot," (they are getting nervous) because the trial has stirred things up, and they're not sure of the outcome. In a monologue, Drummond tells Cates an anecdote about a rocking horse named Golden Dancer that he received as a child. Outside the horse was beautiful, but inside, the wood was rotten. The moral of the story, Drummond says, is, if you discover a lie, " . . . show it up for what it really is." The story of Golden Dancer is analogous both to the creation story as a literal interpretation of events and to the Butler Law. Both, when unexamined, appear unflawed.

The courtroom is "charged with excitement" as the jury returns. Cates is found guilty. The reaction of the spectators is unexpectedly mixed; some clap, some say "Amen," and some boo. Again, Hornbeck provides comic relief as he mocks the verdict by pretending to sell tickets for the Middle Ages and the coronation of Charlemagne.

Cates makes a statement to the court in which he vows to continue to oppose the Butler Law, which he considers unjust. The judge fines Cates a mere $100. According to the stage directions, "the mighty Evolution Law explodes with the pale puff of a wet firecracker." The Butler Law remains a law, but it is now meaningless. Lawrence and Lee refer to the death of McCarthyism—like the Butler Law, it also fizzled out.

Brady wins the trial, but the victory isn't enough; "the prize is his, but he can't reach for the candy." He is angry and in disbelief about Cates' minimal fine. Brady becomes more agitated when he is not given the opportunity to make his closing statement. He tries to give the speech after the court is adjourned, but the confusion in the courtroom, the lack of attention of the spectators, and the intrusion of hawkers selling refreshments make delivering his speech nearly impossible. Then, when the radioman takes his microphone and leaves in mid-oration, Brady is moved beyond embarrassment and anger. The catastrophe of the play occurs when Brady collapses and begins to recite "undelivered inaugural speeches" and soon after dies.

When Cates expresses confusion regarding whether he won or lost, Drummond tells him that he "smashed a bad law," and "made it a joke." Cates won a moral victory and " . . . helped the next fella." Through Drummond, Lawrence and Lee emphasize that the fight for freedom of thought is never over. There will always be issues censoring or limiting the freedom to think that must be fought.

When Rachel returns to the courthouse, she is no longer the timid, unsure young woman who feared questioning her father's or her own beliefs. Newly enlightened, she carries in her suitcase and Darwin's *On the Origin of Species,* which she had borrowed from Cates. She admits to Cates and Drummond that she had " . . . never really thought very much," but realizes that thoughts and ideas are necessary.

After learning of Brady's death, Hornbeck continues to denounce him. Drummond defends Brady, telling Hornbeck that he doesn't have a right to "spit" on Brady or Brady's religion. Hornbeck continues to mock Brady and, composing an obituary for him, Hornbeck realizes that Brady " . . . delivered his own obituary." Looking in a Bible for the proverb that Brady recited at the prayer meeting in Act II, Hornbeck is shocked when Drummond recites the proverb from memory, "He that troubleth his own house shall inherit the wind: and the fool shall be servant to the wise in heart." Then Drummond repeats the plea for tolerance when he tells Hornbeck that Brady had the same right as Cates—"the right to be wrong." Hornbeck realizes that Drummond is more religious than Brady was.

Theme

Through Rachel's growth and Drummond's defense of Brady, as well as his leaving the courthouse with both the Bible and Darwin's *On the Origin of Species,* Lawrence and Lee emphasize the theme of the play: Differing perspectives should be allowed to exist side by side within society.

Glossary

melange a mixture or medley; hodgepodge.

Moorish African people of mixed Berber and Arabic heritage. During the eight century, they conquered much of Spain and Portugal. Under their influence, science, philosophy, and architecture flourished.

people's shoes are getting hot people are getting nervous.

lugging carrying or dragging (something heavy).

precedent an act, statement, legal decision, case, etc. that may serve as an example, reason, or justification for a later one.

hullaballoo loud noise and confusion; hubbub.

gettin' all steamed up becoming angry.

break down a lot of walls to enact change resulting in progress.

cavalcade any procession.

Coronation of Charlemagne Charlemagne (Charles the Great) (742-814) built a huge empire in Europe during the Middle Ages. He was well known for his military victories, the size of his empire, and his respect for Christian doctrine and the law. Charlemagne was coronated on Christmas Day, 800 A.D, in Old Saint Peter's Basilica in Rome.

explodes with the pale puff of a wet firecracker is anticlimactic.

mete to allot; distribute; apportion: usually with *out.*

sine die without (a) day (being set for meeting again); for an indefinite period.

seventh inning stretch a baseball tradition by which people stand up and stretch between the top and bottom of the seventh inning.

sotto voce in an undertone, so as not to be overheard.

cussedness perversity; stubbornness.

Excalibur the magic sword claimed by King Arthur, which only he could remove from the rock in which it was embedded.

rotogravures a printing process using photogravure cylinders on a rotary press.

Corinthians two epistles, letters adopted as books of the New Testament, written by Saint Paul to the church in Corinth, an ancient Greek city.

CHARACTER ANALYSES

Matthew Harrison Brady

Brady is a well-known politician (he ran for the presidency of the United States three times), an excellent orator, a fundamentalist, and a leader of the crusade against the theory of evolution. When he learns the Butler Law is being challenged in Hillsboro, he volunteers to prosecute the defendant, Cates. Brady's mission is to make an example of Cates and to defend the "Living Truth of the Scriptures." When he arrives in Hillsboro with his wife, Sarah, and is greeted by a large crowd of townspeople and the mayor, he "basks in the cheers and the excitement."

Brady's character represents that of William Jennings Bryan, who was the prosecuting attorney for the Scopes trial. Although similarities exist—Bryan was a brilliant politician (he also ran for the presidency three times), a great orator (known as The Great Commoner), a fundamentalist, and a leader of the crusade against teaching Darwin's theory of evolution as truth in public schools—significant differences exists. For example, unlike Brady, Bryan was not out to get Scopes, he was familiar with Darwin's theories, and he did not fall apart on the witness stand. Nor was Bryan the narrow-minded, pompous, hypocrite that is depicted in Brady; in fact, Bryan was known as a cooperative, kind, and charming man.

Lawrence and Lee describe Brady as a large man who appears to be self-confident, kindly, and gracious. "He is gray, balding, paunchy, an indeterminate sixty-five." As he begins to speak to the crowd that meets him at the train, Brady's personal magnetism is obvious; the crowd is in awe of him, and the mayor bestows upon him a commission as Honorary Colonel in the State Militia. Brady is impressed with his new title and the adulation he receives.

Brady questions the townspeople about Cates and uses his favorable reputation to encourage Rachel, a friend of Cates and daughter of Reverend Brown, to trust him and tell him about Cates. He is hypocritical because he acts gently toward Rachel in order to get the information he wants, but once he has that information, he disregards her feelings and requires her to appear as a witness for the prosecution. When she is on the witness stand, he forces her to divulge private conversations she had with Cates. When she becomes distraught, Brady appears unaffected, underscoring the fact that he is simply using her to make an example of Cates.

Brady, the hero of the common people, looks forward to the trial. In that he never questions whether he can win the case or his own position in the battle, he displays *hubris,* or overreaching pride. He arrogantly uses every opportunity to pontificate, to express his opinions. He is certain that he is on the "right" side—the side of fundamentalism—and he sees the trial as a challenge in which he can "test the steel of (his) Truth against the blasphemies of science." As the trial begins, Brady "sits grandly . . . with benign self-assurance." He is confident because the majority of the spectators in the courtroom revere him, and he has their total support.

Brady's character is dynamic, changing as the action of the play unfolds. He is unaware that he has become overzealous about denouncing evolution. Ironically, when he hears Reverend Brown pray for retribution for his own daughter, Brady steps forward and tells him that, "it is possible to be overzealous, to destroy that which you hope to save—so that nothing is left but emptiness." And then he quotes from the Book of Proverbs: "He that troubleth his own house . . . shall inherit the wind."

When Brady is left alone with Drummond after the prayer meeting, he questions Drummond about the friendship they'd once shared. Drummond tells Brady that "perhaps (he has) moved away—by standing still." Brady is shocked. He has been carried by the wave of his popularity and has not stopped to think or to assess his position in relation to changes taking place in American society.

When Drummond calls Brady to the witness stand as an expert on the Bible, "Brady moves to the witness stand in a grandiose style." He is overconfident, underestimating Drummond's shrewd courtroom tactics. In his arrogance, Brady does not think about the consequences of taking the witness stand. Throughout Drummond's questioning, Brady admits that has never read Darwin's evolutionary theories, and it becomes evident that he does not interpret the Bible literally but instead thinks, as God intended man to do. In this scene, Brady is transformed from a strong, confident leader to a pathetic, floundering fool. In his public humiliation and the destruction of his credibility, he becomes a tragic character.

Brady wins the case, but his victory is bitter. When his closing speech is interrupted and eventually cut short by inattentive spectators, he loses the last quality that, until now, had been unassailable: his ability to communicate. Unable to accept being ignored and laughed at, Brady collapses and ultimately dies.

Henry Drummond

Henry Drummond, the *deuteragonist*, or character second in importance in *Inherit the Wind*, can be considered the hero of the play. Functioning as the mouthpiece for Lawrence and Lee, Drummond fights for man's right to think as well as "the right to be wrong." He saves the townspeople of Hillsboro from their narrow-minded fundamentalist views.

In comparison to the Scopes trial, Drummond represents Clarence Darrow, who was the defense attorney for John Scopes. Both Darrow and the character of Drummond are similar in appearance, defend the underdog, put the prosecuting attorney on the witness stand, and lose the trial only to immediately appeal the verdict. Darrow, however, unlike Drummond, had a hostile demeanor and was sarcastic and condescending. His reason for defending Scopes was to expose the ignorance of fundamentalism; Drummond's mission is to find the truth.

Drummond is a "slouching hulk of a man." He is bent over and his head juts forward. He dresses fashionably and is evidently a sophisticated man from the North. He is idealistic and claims to be an agnostic, believing that knowing whether God exists isn't possible. Drummond has been sent to Hillsboro at the request of the Baltimore *Herald* to defend Cates. He is an intelligent, shrewd, and skilled courtroom attorney, well known for defending notorious criminals. He agrees to defend Cates because he believes in freedom of thought.

Given the portrayal of the townspeople, their initial reaction to the news that Drummond is defending Cates alerts the audience to the fact that Drummond is the antithesis to the values that are entrenched in Hillsboro. This dichotomy is most apparent when Melissa, a young girl, first sees him and screams that he is the devil.

Unfazed at being shunned by the townspeople, Drummond is self-confident and charming in the courtroom. He speaks in a folksy tone of voice, albeit businesslike and purposeful, and reveals his sense of humor. For example, he laughs about his purple suspenders, evidence that he is a nonconformist and, as such, different from the residents of Hillsboro.

During the trial, Drummond's sensitive and caring demeanor for his client and his passion for justice become evident. He is angry when Brady is referred to as "Colonel" for no apparent reason, a situation that is prejudicial to his case. When the judge and mayor of Hillsboro bestow a temporary honorary title on him, Drummond appears "politely amused." He is adamant about wanting a fair trial and jurors who can think for themselves, not jurors who "are run through a meat-grinder so they all come out the same." Drummond's goal is to prevent narrow-minded people from altering the Constitution of the United States with old-fashioned nonsense. He is empathetic toward Cates and his lonely situation. He is committed to defending Cates and respects Cates for "standing up when everybody else is sitting down."

When the judge tells Drummond that he cannot call his witnesses, the audience sees Drummond's quick mind, his ability to function under pressure, and his creativity. Changing tactics, he calls Brady, the prosecuting attorney, to the witness stand as an expert on the Bible. Although unorthodox, the situation is particularly significant because it pits one great man against another.

Drummond's character serves as a foil for Brady's character. This function becomes particularly evident during Drummond's cross-examination of Brady. Drummond's patient demeanor and open-minded, progressive way of thinking accentuates Brady's narrow-minded way of thinking. By hammering away at the inconsistencies and eventually attacking Brady's self-anointed status of prophet, Drummond is able to sway the spectator's support in his direction, to open their eyes to truth. As he tells Cates the story of Golden Dancer, the rocking horse that was "all shine and no substance," he makes clear that the true hero is one who discloses lies and stands up for truth.

Even though Cates is found guilty, Drummond wins a moral victory. He reveals his integrity when he defends freedom of thought, even for those he disagrees with. When Hornbeck criticizes Brady and Brady's fundamentalist beliefs, Drummond tells Hornbeck that " . . . Brady had the same right as Cates: the right to be wrong!"

Drummond is a static character; he does not change during the action of the play. At the play's beginning, Drummond is in Hillsboro to defend freedom of thought, and he has little patience for narrow-minded people who criticize the beliefs of others. At the end of the play, Drummond feels the same way and is still fighting for people's "right to be wrong."

E. K. Hornbeck

In his mid thirties, E.K. Hornbeck is a brilliant newspaper columnist for the Baltimore *Herald* and is sent to Hillsboro to cover Cates' trial. His character shares traits with H. L. Mencken, a newspaper columnist for the Baltimore *Sun* who covered the Scopes trial. Although Hornbeck, like Mencken, is cynical, insolent, and flippant, he is not malicious. He is, he admits, "admired for his detestability." In addition, Hornbeck's character is insightful, finding humor in sensitive issues such as evolution and religion. His sense of humor provides comic relief throughout the trial, alleviating the tension that builds as the townspeople try to hold onto traditional beliefs.

Hornbeck is contemptuous of the bigotry and ignorance that seems to exist in southern society. From the moment Hornbeck arrives in Hillsboro, his air of superiority is obvious. He "sneers politely at everything," and his clothes are "those of a sophisticated city-dweller." He speaks haughtily, as though he is reciting poetry; in fact, Lawrence and Lee use verse for Hornbeck's lines. Hornbeck is a *chorus character*. His wisecracks are comments on the action in the play, as well as a representation of progressive ideas and beliefs held by people from the North. He mocks the people of Hillsboro for their fundamentalist beliefs and their narrow-minded views about evolution. He acknowledges that "a few ignorance bushes" exist in Hillsboro, but no "tree of knowledge." He sees a monkey and calls it "Grandpa" and buys a hot dog instead of a Bible because he chooses to feed his stomach rather than his soul.

Hornbeck ridicules Brady for his bigotry and backwardness. Because Brady was a politician and ran for the presidency of the United States three times before becoming a staunch defender of fundamentalism, Hornbeck calls him "a shouter," "an also-ran," "a might-have-been, an almost-was." He claims that Brady came to Hillsboro to find a stump to shout from, not to be the "champion of ordinary people." Hornbeck thinks Brady is a fraud and continues to denounce him even after Brady dies. Hornbeck also enjoys informing the citizens of Hillsboro that the agnostic, Henry Drummond, " . . . the most agile mind of the Twentieth Century," will be defending Cates.

In contrast to his feelings towards Brady and the people of Hillsboro, Hornbeck, who supports evolutionary theory, is supportive of Cates and his courage to stand up for his beliefs. Feeling smug, Hornbeck also pays Cates' bond of $500 at the conclusion of the trial.

Hornbeck's character is static. He is as opinionated and iconoclastic, attacking institutions and firmly held beliefs, and he does not change throughout the course of the play. His character is also shallow and one-dimensional. Because he is first and foremost a newspaper columnist, he is talkative and always in everyone else's business, asking questions and speaking his mind. At the end of the play, when he realizes that Drummond just might be more religious than Brady claimed to be, his immediate reaction is to locate a typewriter to "hammer out (a) story."

Bertram Cates

Cates is a modest, quiet, unpretentious 24 year old. The stage directions describe him as a "pale, thin young man" who is "not particularly good looking." He is a static character; a character who doesn't change throughout the play. Even though things happen *to* Cates, his character is the same at the end of the play as it is at the beginning.

Cates, who clearly represents John Scopes, is the defendant. Although they share the same role, that of defendant, Scopes volunteered to be arrested so that the Butler Law could be tested and never went to jail. The people in Dayton also never shunned Scopes; in fact, his teaching position was still open to him after the trial.

Cates spends the duration of the trial in jail. Never having been in any kind of trouble before, he is frightened, and, even though he is morally innocent and unrepentant, he is unprepared for the reaction of the townspeople. Because he is a proud man, he is embarrassed to have Rachel see him in jail. His strength of character is evident when he portrays a sense of humor to put her at ease. He jokes about the quality of food in jail as compared to the awful food at the boarding house where he's been living and the crime wave that would take place each summer if everyone knew how cool it was in the jail. When Rachel pressures him to admit that what he did (teach evolution to his sophomore science class) was wrong, Cates doesn't get angry or defensive. He simply tries to explain to her that "It isn't as simple as that. Good or bad, black or white, night or day." Cates is disappointed because Rachel doesn't understand what it means to think freely. Rachel is only aware of the fundamentalist beliefs that her father has forced upon her.

The circus-like atmosphere that surrounds the trial and the changes that Cates perceives in the people of Hillsboro both shock and sadden him. He "never thought it would be . . . like Barnum and Bailey (a circus) coming to town." Cates is observant and perceptive. People in the community treat him as though he is a murderer, as if he "had horns growing out of his head." Even his friends turn their backs on him. His reputation and respectability are slowly being destroyed. Despite his situation and the loneliness that he feels, Cates is determined to stand up for what he believes.

When Rachel testifies against Cates during the trial, he feels betrayed and scared because she reveals private conversations they shared. He is also angry because the truth is twisted in support of fundamentalism. Because Cates cares about Rachel, he puts his own interests and feelings aside and forgives her when he sees how distraught she is on the witness stand. He tells Drummond, "Don't plague her. Let her go."

Although the jury finds Cates guilty, he remains idealistic. In his statement to the court, he vows to continue to oppose the Butler Law in any way he can. He is proud of himself for standing up for academic freedom. He is also proud of Rachel when she arrives at the courthouse and shares her realization about how having the freedom to think is important. Cates and Rachel leave Hillsboro together.

Rachel Brown

Rachel Brown, the 22-year-old daughter of Reverend Jeremiah Brown, is a "pretty, but not beautiful" girl. She is a kind and gentle person who dislikes controversy. Rachel is a second-grade schoolteacher and close friend of Bert Cates. She is a purely fictitious character created by Lawrence and Lee. She has no counterpart in the Scopes trial.

Rachel is a dynamic character, a character that is transformed by her experiences and actions. The audience is first introduced to Rachel as she visits Cates in jail. She is nervous and unsure of herself because she has never been to the jail before and because she knows that her father would disapprove of her visiting Cates. Rachel meets Cates and tries to persuade him to admit that he was wrong to teach evolution to his students. She wants him to be on the "right side of things," the side her father is on, the side of fundamentalism.

Rachel's father, a zealous fundamentalist preacher, raised her, and she learned at a young age to fear her father and any thoughts she ever had that deviated from fundamentalism. For Rachel, it had always been " . . . safer not to think at all." She is confused because she loves Cates who believes in academic freedom, yet academic freedom (freedom of thought) is in opposition to her fundamentalist beliefs (a strict interpretation of the Bible).

Rachel questions her own beliefs as she gains awareness of the respect that Drummond and Hornbeck have for Cates. Later, when her father holds a prayer meeting and prays that Cates be destroyed, Rachel automatically defends Cates, only to have her father call for retribution against her also. Disappointed and disillusioned, Rachel must face the fact that her father and his beliefs—and embarrassingly her own beliefs—are narrow-minded and intolerant.

When Rachel testifies against Cates, the stage directions compare her to Brutus, a character in Shakespeare's *Julius Caesar* who betrays his friend Caesar. By testifying, Rachel betrays Cates. The situation becomes unbearable for Rachel when she is on the witness stand, and it results in her near breakdown.

After reading *On the Origin of Species* by Darwin, Rachel admits to Cates and Drummond that she doesn't agree with the theory of evolution but realizes and understands the importance of having the freedom to think. Rachel acts on her newfound awareness by leaving her father and his influence over her. She leaves Hillsboro with Cates.

CRITICAL ESSAYS

Dramatic Conventions and Devices

To reveal information about characters and events in *Inherit the Wind*, Lawrence and Lee utilize a number of dramatic conventions and devices. They use a *foil*, a sharp contrast between two characters, to enhance the characteristics of Brady and Drummond. *Monologue*, a speech given by one person without interruption, is used to expose aspects of Drummond's personality. A *romance motif*, a conventional subplot, develops concerning Rachel and her love for Cates despite their differing viewpoints. Hornbeck's cynicism and wit, in the form of poetry, creates the effect of a *chorus character*. Finally, the Southern *dialect* spoken by the townspeople emphasizes the difference between the North and South and between rural and cosmopolitan areas. These dramatic conventions and devices advance the plot of *Inherit the Wind*.

Foil

Lawrence and Lee place Drummond, the defense attorney, and Brady, the prosecuting attorney, side by side, thereby dramatizing the differences between the two characters. In Act II, Scene 2, when Brady takes the witness stand, it becomes apparent that Drummond serves as a foil for Brady. Drummond remains patient and methodical as he cross-examines Brady, but Brady becomes frustrated, confused, and bitter. Each character is intensified by the presence of the other, and their differences are magnified. As Brady crumbles, Drummond becomes the hero of the townspeople, saving them from censored knowledge and narrow-minded thinking.

Monologue

When the audience first learns that Drummond, the famous defense attorney for underdogs, will be arriving in Hillsboro, the impression Lawrence and Lee create is that of a hardened, no-nonsense man who is defending Cates to serve his own purposes. The playwrights use monologue, a long uninterrupted speech in the presence of others, to portray Drummond's true character. At the end of Act I, Scene 2, Drummond tells Cates and Rachel that he understands the loneliness Cates is feeling. He is empathetic. Drummond clearly values honesty and believes in standing up for one's beliefs. In Act II, Scene 2, Drummond addresses the court, adamantly relating his belief that, "An idea is a greater monument than a cathedral." He cares deeply about the freedom of the individual human mind and understands the price that must be paid for progress. Finally, in Act III, Drummond tells Cates his story about Golden Dancer. In it, he reveals his never-ending search for truth. At the end of the play, the audience has a different impression of Drummond's character. He is a hero who opens people's eyes to the value of freedom of thought and the need to fight censorship.

The Romance Motif

Lawrence and Lee use a romance motif, a conventional subplot, to portray the conflict between bigotry and enlightenment. Rachel, the daughter of a fundamentalist preacher, falls in love with Cates, an evolutionist. Rachel is torn between her own fundamentalist beliefs and love for her father and her love for Cates. At first, she wants Cates to change his plea, to admit he was wrong.

At the welcome picnic for Brady and at her father's prayer meeting, Rachel is confronted with situations involving devout fundamentalists causing her to question her own fundamentalist beliefs. Brady, a man whom she respects and trusts, manipulates her into revealing confidential conversations she had with Cates and forces her to testify against Cates in court. Later, during a prayer meeting, her father condemns Cates, and Rachel as well, when she speaks out in support of Cates.

Rachel knows Cates is not a bad person because he has different beliefs. She reads Darwin's evolutionary theory and draws her own conclusions. As she tells Cates and Drummond, "I was always afraid of what I might think—so it seemed safer not to think at all . . . now I know . . . if (an idea) dies inside you, part of you dies, too!" Rachel becomes enlightened and leaves Hillsboro with Cates.

Chorus Character

A dramatic convention Lawrence and Lee use to portray a benighted South is a chorus character—a Greek chorus reduced to one character. In classic Greek drama, the chorus sings its lines as it comments on the action of the play and predicts the future of the characters. In *Inherit the Wind*, Hornbeck's character has the effect of being a chorus character. His lines, written in the form of poetry, allow him to function as a commentator. He is a vehicle for comic relief as he moralizes and relays information to the audience. Hornbeck is amused at the lack of sophistication and narrow-mindedness he observes in Hillsboro. He mocks

Hillsboro, the residents, their fundamentalist beliefs, and their leader, Brady, throughout the play. In Act I, Scene 1, he comments to a community member:

"The unplumbed and plumbing-less depths!

Ahhhh, Hillsboro—Heavenly Hillsboro.

The buckle on the Bible Belt."

He tells Rachel that there are "A few ignorance bushes (in Hillsboro) . . .(but) No Tree of Knowledge." He makes fun of fundamentalism when he sees a monkey and exclaims, "Grandpa!" Hornbeck claims that Brady arrived in Hillsboro "to find himself a stump to shout from. That's all." He did not show up to be the "champion of ordinary people." After Brady dies, Hornbeck says:

"How do you write an obituary

For a man who's been dead thirty years?"

Hornbeck's commentary on the fundamentalists in Hillsboro illustrates the perceived differences that exist between the North and South and between cosmopolitan and rural areas within the United States.

Dialect

Lawrence and Lee use a southern dialect to realistically portray the residents of Hillsboro, as well as to illustrate their lack of sophistication. A dialect is a spoken version of a language. Dialects are regional and are often class languages having distinct features of pronunciation, grammar, and vocabulary. Southern dialect is informal, using figurative language and colorful expressions. For example, in Act I, Scene 1, Howard asks Melinda, "What're yuh skeered of?" As the townspeople prepare for Brady's arrival, the audience hears that the paint on the banner, "didn't dry 'til jist now," the picnic the women prepared is "Fitt'n fer a King," and because of Brady's arrival, the "Town's gonna fill up like a rain barrel in a flood."

Lawrence and Lee use the Southern dialect spoken by the people of Hillsboro to stereotype the townspeople as "ignorant Southerners." This implication leads to the theme of the play and the conflict between evolutionism (progressive thinking) and fundamentalism or creationism (reactionary thinking).

Lawrence and Lee use conventions and devices to emphasize the themes of the play: Knowledge must not be censored, people must fight for freedom of thought, and differing beliefs must be valued. Although the playwrights based *Inherit the Wind* on the 1925 Scopes trial, it was published and produced in 1955, in the midst of the McCarthy era, and as they state, the setting, " . . . might have been yesterday. It could be tomorrow."

Themes

When considering the themes of *Inherit the Wind*, the student should keep in mind that the play was first published in 1955, *not* 1925 when the Scopes trial took place. During the early 1950s, known as the McCarthy era, actors and writers were blacklisted—that is, refused work because they had been accused of having some connection to Communism.

During this period, people stopped expressing their thoughts, beliefs, or ideas, afraid they would lose their livelihood or worse. Being writers, Lawrence and Lee became aware of the dangerous situation created when laws are passed limiting the freedom to think and speak. When writing *Inherit the Wind*, the playwrights were not concerned with the controversy between evolution and creation, the focus of the Scopes trial. Instead, they were concerned with the censoring or limiting of an individual's freedom to think. The authors used the issue of evolution as a metaphor for control over an individual's thoughts or beliefs. *Inherit the Wind*, then, is Lawrence and Lee's response to the McCarthy era.

Freedom of Thought

The predominant theme in *Inherit the Wind* is freedom of thought. Cates, like Scopes, is arrested for violating the Butler Law, which prohibits teaching evolutionary theory in public schools in Tennessee, effectively censoring what could be taught in public school classrooms. Drummond, Lawrence and Lee's voice throughout the play, fights passionately against censoring knowledge. When knowledge is censored, the right to think is limited. Drummond is adamant about everyone having the right to think. When Brady accuses Drummond of " . . . destroying everybody's belief in the Bible, and in God," Drummond responds, "You know that's not true. I'm trying to stop you bigots and ignoramuses from controlling the education of the United States."

Another issue important to Lawrence and Lee is tolerance for different or conflicting beliefs. At the conclusion of the play, Hornbeck continues to denounce Brady after his death. Drummond vehemently tells him that, ". . . You have no more right to spit on his religion than you have a right to spit on my religion! Or my lack of it! . . . Brady had the same right as Cates: the right to be wrong!"

In a society that honors freedom of thought, it is necessary to value beliefs that differ from one's own. Even though Drummond is referring to the evolutionist/fundamentalist conflict in *Inherit the Wind,* the issue of intolerance and lack of respect for differing beliefs and thoughts is evident during the McCarthy era as well. People's lives were ruined for even the slightest connection to Communism. Drummond's comment, "the right to be wrong," is a plea that was common to the McCarthy era.

Another major theme in *Inherit the Wind* is the value of every person's ability to think and have ideas. The message that Lawrence and Lee convey through Drummond is that when people think and have ideas, they are not standing still. An idea to Drummond " . . . is a greater monument than a cathedral." The authors believe people need to be shaken up, confronted with new information, knowledge, and ideas so they can think independently and not merely conform with the majority or most popular opinion. Drummond tells the court that he is trying " . . . to prevent the clock-stoppers [the fundamentalists] from dumping a load of medieval nonsense [the Butler Law] into the United States Constitution." Lawrence and Lee convey the message that people must stand up and continue to fight against laws that promote censorship and unthinking conformity. Drummond tells Cates that the fight for freedom is never finished.

Search for Truth

Truth is another theme important to Lawrence and Lee. When Drummond defends Cates in the courtroom, he is seeking the truth. He tells the courtroom that "right" and "wrong" have no meaning to him; only " . . . Truth has meaning." Lawrence and Lee convey their respect for differing perspectives: Neither evolutionism nor fundamentalism is right or wrong. At the conclusion of the play, Drummond walks off with both a Bible and a copy of Darwin's *On the Origin of Species* in his brief case.

Lawrence and Lee's belief in a continuing search for truth is represented in Drummond's Golden Dancer speech to Cates. He tells Cates to " . . . look behind the paint . . . if it's a lie—show it up for what it really is." The authors are referring to the Butler Law, as well as the McCarthy era blacklisting.

Lawrence and Lee urge their audiences to pay attention to what is going on around them; to protect their freedoms by thinking, having ideas, and searching for truth. Only by being open-minded and respecting differing beliefs and viewpoints can freedoms be guaranteed.

Conflicts in *Inherit the Wind*

The themes of *Inherit the Wind*—the necessity of freedom of thought and the value of seeking the truth—are revealed through the many conflicts in the play. The obvious conflict, that between Drummond and Brady, most obviously highlights these themes, but Lawrence and Lee include other conflicts, both external and internal, as well. The conflicts that their characters face in *Inherit the Wind* give the audience an appreciation for the value of ideas, the need for mutual respect regarding differing perspectives, and the importance of the freedom to think.

External Conflicts

The focus of *Inherit the Wind* is the external conflict between Brady and Drummond. The conflict has been referred to as "the legal battle of the [twentieth] century." Brady, the prosecuting attorney, is on the side of creationism. He is fighting in favor of the Butler Law, which prohibits teaching evolutionary theory in public classrooms in Tennessee. Drummond, Cates' defense attorney, is on the side of evolutionism. He is opposed to the Butler Law because the freedom to think is jeopardized when knowledge is censored.

At one time, the men had been good friends. They admired and understood each other until their opposing beliefs caused them to become adversaries. The conflict between Brady and Drummond is resolved in the play. Brady wins the trial, and Drummond wins a moral victory. Because Cates stood up for what he believed—that it is right to teach evolutionary theory to students—a bad law was "smashed" and Cates has "helped the next fella" who decides to stand up and fight.

The conflict between Brady and Drummond is not just a conflict between two men and their beliefs. Their battle represents conflicts that exist within American society—for example, the continuing conflict between evolutionism and creationism, modernists versus fundamentalists, church versus state, and agnosticism versus faith. Conflicts arise when people do not value or respect differing beliefs. Lawrence and Lee use the conflict between Brady and Drummond to convey the need to fight for the freedom to think and the need to respect differing perspectives.

Lawrence and Lee also bring awareness to cultural conflicts by presenting the differing perspectives between the North and South and between cosmopolitan and rural areas through the external conflict faced by Hornbeck. Hornbeck, a sophisticated newspaper columnist from the city, detests being in Hillsboro, "The buckle on the Bible Belt." He can't wait to get back to civilization (Baltimore, in the North). Even his clothes "contrast sharply with the attire of the townspeople" who live in the rural south. Hornbeck continuously mocks rural Southern society for its ignorance and bigotry and, in contrast, comments on the progressive ideas and beliefs held by people living in cosmopolitan areas of the North.

The conflict Cates experiences is also external. He has violated the Butler law because he taught evolutionary theory to students in a public school in Tennessee. Cates is in jail and is fighting for his freedom and, ultimately, for the repeal of the Butler Law. Cates' conflict is representative of the conflict that exists between collective versus individual rights—in this case, the government of the state of Tennessee versus Cates and his belief that the Butler Law is unjust because it violates his Constitutional rights.

Internal Conflicts

Brady also experiences an internal conflict. He is a dynamic character who changes during the course of the play due to his experiences. When the play begins, Brady is self-confident and arrogant. He is leader of the common people, and he basks in his popularity. He is sure that fundamentalism is right and evolutionism is wrong. As the trial progresses and Brady takes the witness stand to be cross-examined by Drummond, his character changes. He experiences inner conflict because he is forced to admit that he doesn't interpret the Bible literally, a major fundamentalist tenet. His once loyal followers laugh at him and then ignore him as they turn their backs and walk away. Brady is transformed from a confident leader to a tragic character who, because of his ordeal, dies.

Rachel's internal conflict between fundamentalism and modernism enables the authors to convey their belief in freedom of thought and the value of ideas. Raised a fundamentalist, Rachel loves her father (Reverend Brown) and only knows one way to think. She also loves Cates, a modernist who believes in thinking and in wondering about the world. Rachel's conflict involves her love for her father and her lifelong fundamentalist beliefs and her love for Cates and his different thoughts on life and religion. After reading Darwin's *On the Origin of Species,* Rachel is enlightened. She chooses to think and recognizes the value of ideas—good or bad. As she tells Cates and Drummond, "I was always afraid of what I might think—so it seemed safer not to think at all . . . But now I know . . . A thought . . . has to be born . . . ideas have to come out. . . .." Rachel makes the choice to leave Hillsboro and her father with Cates.

A Note On Proverbs

A proverb is a short, concise statement that presents a moral or a truth about human behavior. Proverbs are most often based on experience, common sense, or observation. Proverbs rely on figurative language such as metaphor, simile, alliteration, or rhyme. Consider the following examples:

- Metaphor: "Don't wash your dirty linen in public."

- Simile: "Experience is the mother of wisdom."

- Alliteration: "Rob Peter to pay Paul."

- Rhyme: "Red sky in morning, sailors take warning."

Proverbs are often written down and can be found in literature. Benjamin Franklin wrote many proverbs and used proverbs from other sources in his *Poor Richard's Almanac,* and Miguel de Cervantes *Don Quixote* includes proverbs. Probably the most well known written proverbs are found in the Book of Proverbs in the Old Testament of the Bible. The Book of Proverbs is a collection of moral and philosophical sayings. Previously thought to be written entirely by King Solomon, son of David, scholars have determined that the material comes from different periods in the history of ancient Israel.

The Proverbs are teachings, practical guidance for daily living intended to benefit individuals and communities. Because they are meant to be repeated, they are short and easily remembered. They are written as parallelisms, a pattern common in Hebrew poetry, and are usually couplets (two lines), although in some instances, the parallelism can extend to three or more lines. The meaning of the first line may be reinforced or restated by the second line:

How much better to get wisdom than gold,
    To choose understanding rather than silver!
    (Proverbs 16:16)

In another pattern, the second line states the opposite of the first line:
    He who walks with the wise grows wise,
    but a companion of fools suffers harm.
    (Proverbs 13:20)

In a third pattern, the second line completes the thought of the first:
    A fool finds no pleasure in understanding
    but delights in airing his own opinions.
    (Proverbs 18:2)

The title of *Inherit the Wind* is taken from Proverbs 11:29:
    He that troubleth his own house shall inherit the wind:
    and the fool shall be servant to the wise in heart.

As such, the title of the play is foreboding. When people create problems within their family, community, or country, they ultimately suffer the consequences of their actions. Through this title, the playwrights alert the audience to the coming conflict.

Lawrence and Lee used Proverb 11:29 in two other instances in the play. In Act II, Scene 1, Reverend Brown gives a fire-and-brimstone sermon at a prayer meeting held on the courthouse lawn. He becomes overzealous in condemning Cates, and when his daughter asks him to stop, he asks for retribution for her also. Brady intervenes because he is concerned he will lose the support of the townspeople. The advice he gives to Reverend Brown is the wisdom of Solomon in the Book of

Proverbs, "He that troubleth his own house . . . shall inherit the wind." Brown has caused trouble in his own house by condemning his daughter and will, ultimately, "inherit the wind," when Rachel leaves him.

The second time Lawrence and Lee use Proverb 11:29 is in Act III. Hornbeck comments that when Brady recited Proverb 11:29 to Reverend Brown, he was in fact " . . . delivering his own obituary." Brady "inherited the wind": He died as a result of his actions. He made a mistake believing he was infallible.

The community members cause trouble for themselves because they create a circus-like atmosphere during the trial and in so doing, draw worldwide attention to their narrow-minded views. They "inherited the wind" because, like the townspeople of Dayton after the Scopes trial, their reputation remained that of the stereotypical "ignorant Southern town."

CliffsNotes Review

Use this CliffsNotes Review to test your understanding of the original text and reinforce what you've learned in this book. After you work through the review and essay questions, identify the quote section, and the fun and useful practice projects, you're well on your way to understanding a comprehensive and meaningful interpretation of *Inherit the Wind*.

Q&A

1. Rachel goes to the jail to see Bert because

    a. she loves him

    b. she wants to give him support and shirts

    c. she wants to convince him to to admit he was wrong

2. When Drummond arrives in Hillsboro, what does Melinda mistake him for?

    a. a vagrant

    b. the devil

    c. her visiting uncle

3. When they are alone after the prayer meeting, Drummond implies that Brady

    a. has turned his back on the truth

    b. has chosen to fight for the wrong cause

    c. has moved farther away by standing still

4. Although Brady won the trial, how did he lose?

    a. he has lost the regard of the community and his reputation

    b. the insignificance of the fine implies that the crime (teaching evolution) was also insignificant

    c. he dies

5. A turning point in Rachel's enlightenment is_____.

Answers: (1) a and c. (2) b. (3) c. (4) a, b, and c. (5) Rachel begins to question her own perceptions and assumptions when she realizes that men of high regard (that is, Hornbeck and Drummond) respect Cates and when she, herself, is condemned by her father because she speaks out in Cates' behalf at the prayer meeting.

Identify the Quote

1. . . . they'll crucify me!

2. He that troubleth his own house . . . shall inherit the wind.

3. Perhaps it is *you* who have moved away—by standing still.

4. [E]volution is not on trial.

5. An idea is a greater monument than a cathedral.

Answers: (1) [Bert is speaking to Drummond and Rachel when Rachel reveals that Brady is forcing her to testify about private conversations that she and Cates had.] (2) [In the first instance, Brady quotes this proverb to Reverend Brown and the people at the prayer meeting after Brown condemns his own daughter. In the second instance, after Brady's death, Hornbeck tries to remember the words, finding them a suitable epitaph for Brady. Drummond recalls them for him.] (3) [Drummond is speaking to Brady, when Brady asks what happened to the friendship they shared and implies that Drummond has moved away from him.] (4) [The judge is speaking to Drummond and denying the relevance of Drummond's expert witnesses.] (5) [Drummond is speaking to the court, angrily responding to the claim that he is being contemptuous of all that is holy.]

Essay Questions

1. Discuss the present day significance of *Inherit the Wind* and explain why this play has been called "the greatest courtroom drama of the twentieth century."

2. Compare and contrast the characterization of Brady and Drummond. Explain how the perception of the townspeople reinforces their characterizations.

3. Explain how Brady be considered a tragic figure. In your discussion, consider the idea of *hubris.*

4. Analyze the significance of the setting in *Inherit the Wind*. In doing so, consider the role of the town in the play and Lawrence and Lee's portrayal of Southern fundamentalists.

5. Explain how the conversation between Howard and Melinda serves as an introduction to the basic conflict in the play.

Practice Projects

1. *Inherit the Wind* was first produced on stage in 1955. It was produced as a television movie in 1960 and in 1988, and it was on Broadway again in 1996. Each time the play has been produced, it has been successful. Research each era and describe the historical events that may have contributed to the relevance of each production.

2. Read one of the following works and compare it to *Inherit the Wind:*

- Stephen Vincent Benet's *The Devil and Daniel Webster*
- Arthur Miller's *The Crucible*

3. Lawrence and Lee convey the theme through the characterization of their two main characters: Drummond and Brady. Restage parts of the play, changing only these character's personality traits: Make Drummond arrogant and overly confident; make Brady decent and kind. Discuss how such a change affects the audience's reaction to the characters and the central conflict.

4. Imagine that Drummond is asked to give the eulogy at Brady's funeral. Write the eulogy. Or, if you prefer, assume that you, like Hornbeck, have covered the trial and now must write an article.

5. Create a Web site to introduce *Inherit the Wind* to other readers. Design pages to intrigue and inform your audience, and invite other readers to post their thoughts and responses to their reading of the play.

CliffsNotes Resource Center

The learning doesn't need to stop here. CliffsNotes Resource Center shows you the best of the best—links to the best information in print and online about the author and/or related works. And don't think that this is all we've prepared for you; we've put all kinds of pertinent information at www.cliffsnotes.com. Look for all the terrific resources at your favorite bookstore or local library and on the Internet. When you're online, make your first stop www.cliffsnotes.com where you'll find more incredibly useful information about Inherit the Wind.

Books

This CliffsNotes book provides a meaningful interpretation of Inherit the Wind, published by IDG Books Worldwide, Inc. If you are looking for information about the author and/or related works, check out these other publications:

The Great Monkey Trial, by L. Sprague de Camp, offers a detailed account of the Scopes trial. New York: Doubleday & Company, 1968.

Summer for the Gods, by Edwards J. Larson, offers a retelling of the Scopes trial and the events that led up to it. New York: Basic Books, 1997.

On the Origin of Species by Means of Natural Selection, by Charles Darwin. The reprinted original work that sparked the evolution versus creationism debate. New York: Bantam Classics, 1999.

Contemporary Authors New Revision Series, Vols. 2 and 44. Includes personal information about Jerome Lawrence and Robert E. Lee, their careers, honors and awards, and a detailed list of their published works. Detroit: Gale Research, 1994.

It's easy to find books published by IDG Books Worldwide, Inc. You'll find them in your favorite bookstores (on the Internet and at a store near you). We also have three web sites that you can use to read about all the books we publish:

- ■ www.cliffsnotes.com
- ■ www.dummies.com
- ■ www.idgbooks.com

Internet

Check out these Web resources for more information about Jerome Lawrence, Robert Lee, and Inherit the Wind:

Inherit the Wind Home Page, `http://xroads.virginia.edu/~UG97/inherit/intro.html`—A study of *Inherit the Wind* in chronological order with links to background information, reviews, and contemporary news events.

The Scopes Monkey Trial Home Page, `www.dimensional.com/~randl/scopes.htm`—Includes news clippings and court transcripts of the Scopes trial.

About Jerome Lawrence & Robert E. Lee, `www.lib.ohiostate.edu/OSU_profile/triweb/abtri/lawrence%26lee.html`—Offers biographies of both Jerome Lawrence and Robert E. Lee, as well as photos and images from their plays.

Next time you're on the Internet, don't forget to drop by www.cliffsnotes.com. We created an online Resource Center that you can use today, tomorrow, and beyond.

Magazines and Journals

Couch, Nena. "An Interview with Jerome Lawrence and Robert E. Lee." *Studies in American Drama, 1945-Present.* Vol.7, 1992. 3-18. An interview with Lawrence and Lee via telephone conference call discussing their writing in relation to an exhibit of Lawrence and Lee's work at Ohio State University entitled, "Roughing Up the Consciousness: The Plays of Jerome Lawrence and Robert E. Lee."

_____. "Theater: A Memorable Muni." *Newsweek.* May 2, 1955. A 1955 critical review of *Inherit the Wind.*

"William Jennings Bryan, The Scopes Trial and Inherit the Wind." Internet. www.bryan.edu. March 31, 1999. A detailed biography of Bryan including his personal life, politics, policies and programs, publications and oration, religion, participation in the Scopes trial, and a comparison to Brady, the character that represented Bryan in *Inherit the Wind.*

"Disinherit the Wind." *Nashville Scene.* June 11, 1999. www.weekly-wire.com. An article about the courthouse and courtroom (still in use today) where the Scopes trial took place, along with information about the trial that is not well-known.

Iannone, Carol. "The Truth About Inherit the Wind." *First Things.* April 1, 1999. www.firstthings.com. A comparison of *Inherit the Wind* to the Scopes trial.

"Science v. Religion." *Court TV Online.* June 17, 1999. www.courttv.com. An article about the teaching of evolutionary theory in public schools and the growing fundamentalist movement to put a stop to it.

"The Making of a Trial." *Court TV Online.* June 27, 1999. www.courttv.com. A description of the Scopes trial.

Other Media

New York Times Theater Reviews 1920-1970. Vol. 6, 1971. September 25, 1955, April 22, 1955. Critical Reviews of *Inherit the Wind* from the 1955 stage performance.

"Blacklist." *Microsoft Encarta 98 Encyclopedia.* CD-ROM. Microsoft Corporation: 1993-1997. A description of the blacklist in the entertainment industry during the 1940s and 1950s.

"Darwin, Charles Robert." *Microsoft Encarta 98 Encyclopedia.* CD-ROM. Microsoft Corporation: 1993-1997. A biography of Darwin including information about his voyage aboard the *Beagle*, his theory of natural selection, and reactions to his theory.

"Fundamentalism." *Microsoft Encarta 98 Encyclopedia.* CD-ROM. Microsoft Corporation: 1993-1997. A definition of fundamentalism, as well as the origins and current status.

Lawrence and Lee's Produced Works

Look Ma, I'm Dancin'. By Jerome Lawrence and Robert E. Lee. Composer Hugh Martin. Adelphi Theatre, New York. 1948. A backstage glimpse of a traveling ballet company backed by a beer heiress who insists on performing. The beer heiress becomes a comical "ballerina."

Inherit the Wind. By Jerome Lawrence and Robert E. Lee. National Theatre, New York. 1955. A fictionalized account of the Scopes' trial — a trial based on the importance of an individual's right to the freedom of thought.

Shangri-La. By Jerome Lawrence and Robert E. Lee. Composer Harry Warren. Winter Garden Theatre, New York. 1956. A musical based on *Lost Horizon* by James Hilton, in which three men and one woman are transported to Shangri-La, a mysterious utopia hidden in the mountains of Tibet. The story is a commentary on Western ideals of the 1930s.

Auntie Mame. By Jerome Lawrence and Robert E. Lee. Broadhurst Theatre, New York. 1956. The story of a woman who lives life to the fullest.

The Gang's All Here. By Jerome Lawrence and Robert E. Lee. Ambassador Theatre, New York. 1959. A fictionalized account of the corruption of the presidency of Warren G. Harding.

Only in America. By Jerome Lawrence and Robert E. Lee. Cort Theatre. New York. 1959. Race relations are explored in this play based in part on Harry Golden's life.

A Call on Kuprin. By Jerome Lawrence and Robert E. Lee. Broadhurst Theatre, New York. 1961. Questions of patriotism and the role of the scientist in the modern world are explored using the competition between the American and Soviet space programs.

Mame. By Jerome Lawrence and Robert E. Lee. Winter Garden Theatre, New York. 1966. A musical version of *Auntie Mame.*

Sparks Fly Upward. By Jerome Lawrence and Robert E. Lee. Henry Miller's Theatre (as *Diamond Orchid),* New York. 1956; McFarlin Auditorium, Dallas. 1967. The effects of societal oppression of individual development are explored in this fictionalized account of the life and death of Evita Peron.

The Night Thoreau Spent in Jail. By Jerome Lawrence and Robert E. Lee. Ohio State University, Columbus, Ohio. 1970; Arena Theatre, Washington, DC. 1970. Thoreau is put in jail after refusing to pay taxes to the American government, which at the time was involved in what Thoreau considered an unjust war with Mexico (the Mexican-American War, 1846-48).

First Monday in October. By Jerome Lawrence and Robert E. Lee. Kennedy Center, Washington, DC. 1977; Majestic Theatre, New York. 1978. Censorship is explored in this play about the first woman on the Supreme Court.

Send Us Your Favorite Tips

In your quest for learning, have you ever experienced that sublime moment when you figure out a trick that saves time or trouble? Perhaps you realized you were taking ten steps to accomplish something that could have taken two. Or you found a little-known workaround that gets great results. If you've discovered a useful tip that helped you understand Inherit the Wind and you'd like to share it, the CliffsNotes staff would love to hear from you. Go to our Web site at www.cliffsnotes.com and click the Talk to Us button. If we select your tip, we may publish it as part of CliffsNotes Daily, our exciting, free e-mail newsletter. To find out more or to subscribe to a newsletter, go to on the Web.

INDEX

The Odyssey
Oedipus Trilogy
Of Human Bondage
Of Mice and Men
The Old Man and
   the Sea
Old Testament
Oliver Twist
The Once and
   Future King
One Day in the Life of
   Ivan Denisovich
One Flew Over
   Cuckoo's Nest
100 Years of Solitude
O'Neill's Plays
Othello
Our Town
The Outsiders
The Ox Bow Incident
Paradise Lost
A Passage to India
The Pearl
The Pickwick Papers
The Picture of
   Dorian Gray
Pilgrim's Progress
The Plague
Plato's Euthyphro…
Plato's The Republic
Poe's Short Stories
A Portrait of the
Artist…
The Portrait of a Lady
The Power and
   the Glory
Pride and Prejudice
The Prince
The Prince and
   the Pauper
A Raisin in the Sun
The Red Badge of
   Courage
The Red Pony
The Return of the
   Native
Richard II
Richard III

The Rise of
   Silas Lapham
Robinson Crusoe
Roman Classics
Romeo and Juliet
The Scarlet Letter
A Separate Peace
Shakespeare's
   Comedies
Shakespeare's Histories
Shakespeare's
   Minor Plays
Shakespeare's Sonnets
Shakespeare's Tragedies
Shaw's Pygmalion &
   Arms…
Silas Marner
Sir Gawain…Green
   Knight
Sister Carrie
Slaughterhouse-Five
Snow Falling on Cedars
Song of Solomon
Sons and Lovers
The Sound and the Fury
Steppenwolf &
   Siddhartha
The Stranger
The Sun Also Rises
T.S. Eliot's Poems &
   Plays
A Tale of Two Cities
The Taming of the
   Shrew
Tartuffe, Misanthrope…
The Tempest
Tender Is the Night
Tess of the D'Urbervilles
Their Eyes Were
   Watching God
Things Fall Apart
The Three Musketeers
To Kill a Mockingbird
Tom Jones
Tom Sawyer
Treasure Island &
   Kidnapped

The Trial
Tristram Shandy
Troilus and Cressida
Twelfth Night
Ulysses
Uncle Tom's Cabin
The Unvanquished
Utopia
Vanity Fair
Vonnegut's Works
Waiting for Godot
Walden
Walden Two
War and Peace
Who's Afraid of
   Virginia…
Winesburg, Ohio
The Winter's Tale
The Woman Warrior
Worldly Philosophers
Wuthering Heights
A Yellow Raft in
   Blue Water

Check Out the All-New CliffsNotes Guides

TECHNOLOGY TOPICS

Balancing Your Check-
   book with Quicken
Buying and Selling
   on eBay
Buying Your First PC
Creating a Winning
   PowerPoint 2000
   Presentation
Creating Web Pages
   with HTML
Creating Your First
   Web Page
Exploring the World
   with Yahoo!
Getting on the Internet
Going Online with AOL
Making Windows 98

Work for You
Setting Up a
   Windows 98
   Home Network
Shopping Online Safely
Upgrading and
   Repairing Your PC
Using Your First iMac
Using Your First PC
Writing Your First
   Computer Program

PERSONAL FINANCE TOPICS

Budgeting & Saving
   Your Money
Getting a Loan
Getting Out of Debt
Investing for the
   First Time
Investing in
   401(k) Plans
Investing in IRAs
Investing in
   Mutual Funds
Investing in the
   Stock Market
Managing Your Money
Planning Your
   Retirement
Understanding
   Health Insurance
Understanding
   Life Insurance

CAREER TOPICS

Delivering a Winning
   Job Interview
Finding a Job
   on the Web
Getting a Job
Writing a Great Resume